TOTAL QUALITY

Ron Collard is a partner at Coopers & Lybrand and currently personnel director of Coopers & Lybrand (London). His career began with British Steel in personnel and industrial relations, culminating in full personnel responsibility for the Stanton and Staveley Group – at that time an independent subsidiary.

He joined Coopers & Lybrand in 1982. Initially, he was responsible for developing the people approach to quality and worked with a variety of clients such as Ciba Geigy, Youngs Seafoods, Sony (UK), Gardner Merchant and Shulton (GB), helping them to introduce their quality programmes. He also has wide experience in providing advice and guidance on training and management development to a variety of clients.

He has been a frequent speaker on quality issues within the UK and Europe and has written many articles on the subject, including the first article in *Personnel Management* on quality circles and the Japanese experience. As a result, he has established a national reputation for successfully and practically linking quality programmes with the development of people.

In 1988 Ron Collard was approached by the Institute of Personnel Management to write a book on the principles behind total quality and how organizations could implement a total quality programme to draw the best from their workforce. *Total Quality: Success through people* was first published in 1989 and the second edition was published in 1993. The book was also published in Italy in 1990.

TOTAL QUALITY

success through people

Second Edition

Ron Collard

Institute of Personnel Management

First published 1989
Reprinted 1990 and 1991
Second edition 1993
© Institute of Personnel Management 1989 and 1993

Phototypeset by HBM Typesetting, Chorley, Lancashire
and printed in Great Britain by
Short Run Press Ltd, Exeter, Devon.

British Library Cataloguing in Publication Data

Collard, Ron
    Total Quality: Success Through People. –
    2Rev.ed
    I. Title
    658.300941

ISBN 0–85292–511–5

CONTENTS

Acknowledgements

It is difficult to know where my total quality story starts – perhaps as far back as 1977 when, sponsored by British Steel, I spent a month in the Hoogvens plant of the Dutch Steel Industry and heard for the first time major references to the Japanese way of doing things. I also saw the initial stirrings of the total quality movement in Europe.

In 1981, sponsored through the Gardner Merchant award, I visited Japan and saw directly their approach to quality and people. This provided me with the impetus, backed by the consulting practice of Coopers & Lybrand, to help many clients in the total quality field and gain the experience and knowledge which provided me with the opportunity to write this book. Without the directors, managers and employees of all these client organizations no total quality programme would have been possible. Their commitment, dedication and interest helped to mould my experience and develop the models outlined in the book. My many colleagues within Coopers & Lybrand also provided me with the necessary support, stimulation and guidance to develop the approach.

Total quality is all about success through people. The satisfaction of working with and through so many people in the many and varied organizations has given me a richness of experience which I would not have gained without their help.

Finally I would like to thank Jane and our two children for their patience and understanding through those long weekends of writing. Also my thanks to Morag, my assistant, for her hard work in transcribing and revising the text and making the book possible.

Foreword to Second Edition

The best-selling first edition of *Total Quality: Success through people* provided the definitive approach to total quality. The messages were clear – it takes time, requires total management commitment and it is all about fundamental culture change within organizations.

In the four years since the first edition was published, there have been several important developments in the field of total quality within the UK and Europe. Organizations from many different sectors, public and private, have begun to develop their own total quality programmes. Total quality has spread beyond manufacturing to the service industries and to national and local government. It has even penetrated the merchant banks within the City of London. This extension has coincided with the introduction of the European Quality Award, which establishes, on a European basis, that providing the highest quality service or product is essential to survival in the 1990s and beyond.

Despite all this, the evidence suggests that many organizations will continue to fail to implement total quality successfully or to maintain momentum for their programmes. This second edition takes account of this experience and includes an additional chapter on 'Making it happen'. This points to what needs to be done to prevent failure and reinforces the message throughout the book that total quality can only be applied successfully if it is central to the business strategy and if the people factor is at the core of the approach.

To Jane, Zoe and Liam

PART I

Why Quality?

Chapter 1
THE CHALLENGE TO MANAGEMENT

Everybody agrees that quality is a good thing. Whether you talk of quality of product, quality of service or quality of suppliers, everybody agrees that it should be of the highest standard. This applies within organizations from the highest level. It applies to suppliers, to customers, to users of services – in fact to anyone you may care to ask. And yet, despite this rare unanimity, there is much talk and little action.

The results of a survey by ODI[1] show clearly that top British management consider quality as a survival issue for their organizations (see Figure 1). In fact, all the chief executives interviewed

Figure 1 The Quality Challenge

Executives recognize the critical importance of quality, but most say they must do more to create an environment in which quality can flourish.

98% AGREE STRONGLY	96% AGREE STRONGLY	88% AGREE STRONGLY	17% AGREE STRONGLY
'Quality is now a survival issue for British organizations'	'A reputation for quality is essential for your company's future'	'As a leader of your company you are personally committed to actions designed to ensure and improve quality'	'Your company has done everything to create an environment in which quality work can flourish'

1

strongly agreed that a reputation for quality products and services was essential to their company's survival. Furthermore, as leaders of their company, they were personally committed to actions designed to ensure an improved product or service quality.

And yet, only two out of ten chief executives considered that their company had done everything to create an environment in which quality work could flourish (see Figure 2). In other words,

Figure 2 The Importance of Quality in Competition

Executives say that quality is crucial to their ability to compete against their major competitors.

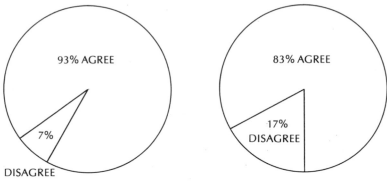

93% AGREE

7%

DISAGREE

'Your company has in place a plan to compete on the basis of quality against your main competition'

83% AGREE

17% DISAGREE

'Organizations today have no choice but to produce a quality product – the competition is just too tough'

the survey confirmed that quality is much talked about but not always followed through sufficiently to ensure success.

The significance of quality is further strengthened by other findings in the survey. Firstly, there is a recognition of the critical importance of quality, since most of top management consider that they must do more to create environments in which quality can flourish. Secondly, there is a recognition that quality is important to customers' buying decisions and that this preoccupation with quality is increasing. Thirdly, quality is considered crucial for organizations to be able to compete against their major competitors.

In organizations of every kind, quality can be regarded as a means to an end – customer satisfaction in all aspects of a product or services. It should be all-pervasive, covering not only the design, performance and reliability of a product or service but the constant improvement of what is on offer.

When it comes to quality, there is often too much emphasis on statistical quality control, quality circles, automation, CAD/CAM and robotics. All are important techniques and processes but at most provide gloss to the total quality programme within an organization. Quality is about attitudes, culture and commitment within an organization. It applies in all organizations: manufacturing, service and public sector, including government. However, quality is also an achievable, measurable and profitable entity that can be introduced into an organization once there is commitment and understanding. As the chief executives in the ODI survey indicated, successful total quality improvement programmes within an organization are related to creating a culture and environment supportive to the continuous improvement of quality.

In quality assurance terms, which are accepted internationally, quality was defined in 1979 as 'the totality of features and characteristics of a product or service that bear on its ability to satisfy a given need'. On this basis, it is possible to evaluate quality first on the criteria of 'fitness of purpose' and second on the 'ability to satisfy a given need', which may include availability, maintainability, reliability and design. In the past, the terms quality assurance, quality control and quality management tended to be used synonymously. British Standards define quality assurance as: 'all activities and functions concerned with the attainment of quality'. This is now widely referred to as total quality control, and related quality systems as total quality management.

In simple terms, quality can be defined as zero defects in the products and services provided by an organization in order to satisfy customer needs. It is about quality in all aspects of company operations and, perhaps even more important, about doing things right first time – which adds nothing to the cost of a company's product or services. Doing things wrong is what costs money.

Quality management is a systematic way of guaranteeing that all activities within an organization happen as planned. It is a management discipline concerned with preventing problems from occurring by creating the attitude and controls that make prevention possible and building a philosophy of continuous improvement. It is also about efficiency, productivity and long-term success.

In summary, I would distinguish between 'quality' defined as the quality of a product or service measured by the extent to which it satisfies the customer, and 'total quality' defined as the culture of an organization where continuous improvement is integrated into all activities.

The attitudes that so often prevail within organizations and affect the quality of the product and services can be encountered every day in the UK. Some years ago I had the opportunity to compare working practices in the steel industry in the UK, Holland and Japan. While in recent years the British steel industry has made a remarkable recovery in terms of efficiency and quality, clear differences in attitudes of mind were apparent at the time.

Housekeeping/cleanliness

I cut my teeth in personnel terms in the UK steel industry, where it was commonly accepted that the nature of the work and the industry were such that it was inevitable that plant and machinery was permanently dirty, old stock was left lying around and it was just too expensive to maintain the highest standards of housekeeping and cleanliness, whether in blast furnaces or rolling mills. It was with some surprise that I visited the Hoogvens steel works in Holland and found a completely different environment and atmosphere. Management started from the position that safe working and high productivity levels were based on good housekeeping standards. Poor standards simply caused breakdowns, accidents and delays in production. This attitude of mind stemmed from top management and was all-pervasive.

Shortly afterwards, I had an opportunity to visit the Nippon steel works on Tokyo Bay. It was almost inconceivable to find yet higher standards of housekeeping and cleanliness, reflecting the total commitment to both safety standards and high productivity levels. Again, top management commitment led the way through a CAP (cost and productivity) programme which continually emphasized the importance of reducing costs and improving productivity; one major aspect of this was the highest standards of housekeeping.

Inspection versus prevention

Productivity standards within the steel industry are measured in terms of output per man. Within a particular rolling mill in the

North East of England, rolling sections for the heavy plant and machinery industry, the measurement was based on tonnage past a particular point in the plant. Plant management, supervision and the workforce concentrated entirely on getting the tonnage through the plant. Management success and the shopfloor productivity bonus were both measured by throughput tonnage. Once rolled, the sections went into the finishing department for cooling, inspection and batching for despatch. With the workforce on a weekly wage package and the emphasis on high productivity bonuses, the concentration of effort was on tonnage with little or no reference to quality. Quality was the responsibility of the inspectors and many long nights were spent arguing whether particular sections should be accepted or rejected. There were times when whole batches were rejected. By the time agreement had been reached on particular rejections, the workforce had been paid their productivity bonus. Why should they care about quality when tonnage was the measure of their bonus and the way management measured their success?

Visits to the Dutch and Japanese plants told a different story. Operators and front-line management were responsible for their own inspection and quality control. In Holland there were no bonus payments at all, with all workers on a monthly salary. Motivation was a management issue and not a question of providing tonnage-based incentives. In Japan there were no short-term bonus payments, although there were annual bonuses reflecting the overall productivity and performance of the organization. In both cases quality standards were maintained by management, supervision and the workforce and there was no incentive to push tonnage through just to get production up.

These attitudes extend to many other industries besides steel.

The preferred customer

When working with a major seafood organization some years ago, I was struck by two production lines producing breaded scampi, one known as the Marks & Spencer line and the other just as Line Number Two. On making further enquiries, I was told that the quality standards which were applied by Marks & Spencer were such that two separate lines were needed. While there was discussion with management about the extra cost of the M & S product, it was clear from a close involvement with the workforce that having two different lines created completely different attitudes to quality. Management had created an environment where the 'preferred customer' had the highest quality standards and demonstrated at all levels in the organization that it was possible to achieve such standards. However, Line Number Two generated a different set of attitudes – 'quality is less important here' – and this pervaded all aspects of the operation. As a result, the actual costs of operation on Line Number Two were considerably in excess of the costs of operation on the M & S line, primarily because of the high reject rate. Management were able to motivate all levels to produce breaded scampi of the highest quality while at the same time (and with the same workforce) producing seriously reduced standards on another line. The question which needed addressing was: 'Are not *all* customers preferred customers?'

Life without customers

I was working on a total quality programme with a major vending organization which provided coffee and food vending machines to their customers, filling and servicing them on a regular basis. Within the programme there was a quality improvement group among the service engineers, who in the early days referred constantly to the problem of the customers. To them the customers were people who damaged machines, who needed haranguing on sensible uses of machines and who were just a plain nuisance. These attitudes also seemed to prevail among management, who regarded the service engineers as a major and expensive overhead, constantly on call to deal with crises 'created by the customer'. Preventative maintenance was a term not used or heard of and, anyway, was 'far too expensive'. A random visit to the machines showed a prevailing attitude of poor servicing and poor quality standards in filling and cleaning the machines. A vicious circle had been created of customers dissatisfied by the quality of service, who probably did not look after the machines well, which in turn aggravated the service engineers, who further upset the customers by their cavalier attitudes. The customer was seen as a threat and a problem rather than as a source of income and profits. The organization's troubles were solely a question of attitudes.

It's not my job

Service organizations rely entirely on good relationships with customers or clients. Within professional firms, initial contacts with clients (as indeed on-going contacts) are often by telephone. While working with a major firm of solicitors, it became apparent to me that telephones ringing out were a major problem which caused huge aggravation within the organization and much dissatisfaction among actual or potential clients. The size and complexity of the organization meant that if you picked up somebody else's phone, it was a long and difficult task to trace the individual required. The result was that nobody would pick up phones, phones would ring out and no doubt many clients were lost.

On one occasion I was talking to a young solicitor who told me that he could never understand that while he was away (which could be for weeks at a time), few new client enquiries would come his way. On his random visits to the office he often received enquiries which could lead to major assignments. It was clear that a climate had been created where there was little or no recognition among the office-based staff of the importance of answering telephones to the business of the organization. The prevailing attitude was 'It's not my job to answer somebody else's telephone because I can't answer or deal easily with the possible clients at the other end of the telephone.' As a result, it was considered better not to answer the phone at all.

The interesting feature was that partners within the organization would also often walk past ringing telephones. It was only when the top management (i.e. the partners) began to set an appropriate example and show their commitment to the changes that people began to accept that it really was their job to answer telephones and respond appropriately.

All these examples demonstrate that total quality is ultimately a management issue. The approach has far less to do with economic or technological considerations than with people and management factors. A total quality programme is to do with changing attitudes, values, beliefs and ways of doing things, and with the prevailing employer/employee relationships within an organization. Management attention needs to be directed at changing these subtle but important issues if quality improvement efforts are to enjoy continued success.

Chapter 2
UNDERSTANDING QUALITY

A great deal has been written about quality management and total quality, but over the last twenty or thirty years a number of key influences and writings can be distinguished as having played a major role. Understanding their approaches and learning from their experiences provides a formidable base from which total quality programmes can be built, developed and tailored within individual organizations.

W. Edwards-Deming

Dr W. Edwards-Deming is probably the father of the quality revolution and provided much of the intellectual drive behind Japan's post-war reconstruction. Within the UK and elsewhere in the West, the belief that improving quality added to costs became received wisdom in the years after the Second World War. The general view was that only a fool would risk adding to costs when, with the great extension of mass-produced consumer goods, the customer expected nothing better. This view has come to be challenged very seriously over the last few years as the Japanese impact on the world market has grown so significantly. It puts the greatest emphasis on efficient use of inputs and can be summarized as follows:

Figure 3 The Traditional Model

Reduce input costs
(ie people, methods, equipment, environment)
↓
Lower unit costs
↓
Increase profit
↓
Improve return on investment
↓
Stay in business

Source: *Personnel Management,* July 1987

With this approach to business, which can achieve short-term returns, quality, because it costs more, is perceived as adversely affecting productivity. Deming challenged this approach and persuaded the Japanese through the Japanese Union of Scientists and Engineers (JUSE) to take up his approach by bringing the customer into the organization and by creating a close link between worker and supplier to work for continuous improvement. Deming's model looks like this:

Figure 4 Deming's Quality-centred Model

Improve quality
↓
Productivity up
↓
Costs down
↓
Prices down
↓
Markets increased
↓
Stay in business
↓
More jobs and better return on investment

Source: *Personnel Management,* July 1987

J. M. Juran

Deming and Juran originally worked closely together in the 1940s; subsequently, Juran's approach has had considerable influence, which he chose to call 'managerial breakthrough'. Juran has argued since the early 1950s that at least 85% of the failures in any organization are the fault of systems controlled by management. Fewer than 15% of the problems are actually worker-related. Management and only management can be responsible for improving the performance of organizations.

Juran's concept of managerial breakthrough distinguishes between what he calls control/inspection and breakthrough or prevention. In a control situation (i.e. traditional management), the *managerial attitude* is one of believing that the present level of performance is good enough or cannot be improved, so the *managerial objective* becomes perpetuating performance at the present level through the control procedure and the *managerial plan* is to identify and eliminate short-lived departures from the usual performance.

In the breakthrough situation, the managerial attitude is one of believing that the present level of performance is not good enough and that something can be done about it. The managerial objective is achieving a better performance and the managerial plan is to identify and eliminate chronic obstacles to this. In other words, Juran also puts the emphasis on continuous improvement.

Juran starts from the position that attitude is the key to managerial breakthrough. There is no change in any organization unless there is first someone to argue for that change. The first step on the road is the belief that a change – a breakthrough – is desirable and feasible in all aspects of operations within an organization in the long term. It is not about short-term results.

One of the difficulties, of course, is that managers simply have no time for 'breakthrough' because they cannot leave the treadmill of 'control'. Few managers would argue against the merits of 'breakthrough', but they do need respite from the never-ending emergencies and crises. Seldom are harassed managers able to work their way out without help from top management and assistance from other specialists.

Recently I was involved in a major quality improvement programme within a 'male toiletries' house. The company had grown rapidly and successfully, achieved a leading position in the marketplace and now wished to consolidate that position. The prevailing managerial style was essentially that of control. A number of major programmes were introduced initially to help top management (and progressively the rest of the organization) develop towards 'breakthrough'. The key component of this programme was a top management workshop to identify more clearly long-term objectives and developments and to strengthen understanding and teamwork. The workshop, which had a high profile throughout the organization, was initially delayed for six months; when it was finally held, it was curtailed because 'there was a major operational crisis'. While we must recognize that crises will always occur, the prevailing attitude was based on controlling the short term without understanding that the short-term pressures were *created* by the lack of 'breakthrough'.

Within the steel industry I often found that, where supervisory manning levels appeared high or excessive (or where there appeared to be large numbers of inspectors), the history was of control problems within a particular plant. The answer to all problems was considered to be: put on more supervision, have more inspectors. Problems were always tackled on the basis of the symptoms rather than trying to look for underlying causes. Juran's basic approach to total quality is to argue that the key to success is overcoming negative attitudes.

Philip B. Crosby

A lot of the pioneering work carried out by both Deming and Juran was done two decades or more ago. Living proof of their success is found primarily in the growth and development of Japanese industry, where quality standards are paramount. Despite this success and the growing threat of competition, the West has in general been slow to recognize not only the importance of quality, but (perhaps more basic than that) the importance of creating an environment or set of attitudes within an organization which promotes continuous improvement and thus the highest quality standards. Peters and Waterman, in their well-known book *In Search of Excellence*, stressed the importance of creating the right attitudes within organizations and quoted extensively from a number of major world organizations which have been successful in promoting positive attitudes to continuous improvement. A more recent major influence on attitudes towards total quality has been Philip Crosby's series of books, in particular *Quality is Free*.[1]

One of the crucial principles espoused by Crosby is that 'in discussing quality we are dealing with a people situation'. His entire approach is based on this particular philosophy and reflects the messages already outlined in discussing the influence of Deming and Juran.

A useful way of measuring the extent to which an organization has begun to integrate quality management into its management processes is to use Crosby's quality management maturity grid. It is based on the concept that there are five stages in quality management maturity:

Uncertainty – when management has no knowledge of quality as a positive management tool

Awakening – when management is beginning to recognize that quality management can help but will not commit resources to it

Enlightenment – when management decide to introduce a formal quality programme

Wisdom – when management and organization reach the stage when permanent changes can be made

Certainty – when quality management is a vital part of organizational management.

Crosby also identified five factors which he considers the absolutes of quality management:

- quality means conformance not elegance
- there is no such thing as a quality problem
- there is no such thing as the economics of quality – it is always cheaper to do the job right first time
- the only performance measurement is the cost of quality
- the only performance standard is zero defects.

These absolutes underlie his approach to a quality improvement programme.

The basic messages from Crosby relate closely to those underlying the approaches of Deming and Juran. In essence, quality starts from a set of attitudes for which management has the major responsibility. Achieving changes in attitudes at all levels within an organization takes time and needs to be managed on a long-term basis.

Chapter 3
THE BRITISH DISEASE

Until comparatively recently (and with the exception of a few major organizations) British industry and commerce did not have a good reputation for quality standards. This was reflected in:

(a) import substitution – Japanese or German goods became more and more synonymous with high quality; it was accepted, for example, that the highest quality cars were always *foreign* cars, an attitude which was not found in much of Europe and certainly not in Japan itself. The cost of this in the balance of payments, let alone jobs and competitiveness, has been enormous; the key problem was the inability of much of British industry and commerce to meet the basic requirement of good quality – meeting customer needs

(b) an attitude whereby shoddy workmanship seemed to be accepted because it was always 'someone else's job' to put it right. A heavy penalty has been paid by much of British industry in not recognizing that quality is more than just inspection

(c) 'workers are to blame' – the general mythology among the buying public and much of management was that the problem was entirely to do with the fact that 'British workers just do not care.' This was often accompanied by comparisons with Japanese workers, who were considered to be compliant, unquestioning and willing to put up with conditions which would be unacceptable in the West. All these attitudes ignored one crucial point – it was a management issue to control and improve quality standards.

(d) resistance to change – much has been written about resistance to change within British industry, but an outstanding example is to be found in the TUC guidelines on quality circles (1981): 'Trade unionists will be opposed to the introduction of QCs if they challenge in any way existing trade union

machinery or practices.' Similarly, management (and particularly middle management) has often resisted changes to working practices on the grounds that since they have been trying to
'run a tight ship' for years, it is difficult for them to accept that
quality standards are not as high as might be expected.

Moving from these general attitudes, we can consider some of
the specific attitudes of managers and employees. Management
attitudes have in the past been characterized by the view that high
quality standards are an ideal – but probably unrealistic. As a
result, management has tended to:

(a) regard quality as an unacceptable expense (as reflected in the
ODI survey already referred to, where everybody agreed that
quality was essential to survival and yet many chief executives
had not done a great deal to change attitudes within their
organizations)

(b) put considerable emphasis on short-term results, which has
meant that the longer term notion of continuous improvement
and investment in total quality programmes has been resisted.
Yet the direct cost of a total quality programme is minute in
relation to the overall benefits likely to come to an organization in the longer term. One of the interesting features of
visiting Japanese companies (such as Canon Cameras) within
Japan and talking about their total quality programme is that
they often find it difficult to recall at what point the organization introduced total quality: the generation who now play a
major role within Japanese industry no longer regard it as
some special or separate aspect of management

(c) follow (or appear to follow) 'flavours of the month'. As long
ago as 1981, I emphasized the particular conditions that
should apply to the introduction of a quality circle programme, especially the need for top management commitment.[1] In the intervening years I have often found that such
commitment has been forthcoming at the *early* stages of a total
quality programme, yet long-term success has only been
achieved if that commitment has also been long term. This
tendency was clearly evident in the male toiletries organization, which launched its total quality programme in the
summer of 1986 and within a relatively short period was
looking for the next major programme to introduce.

Compounding some of the difficulties caused by these management attitudes to quality, employees have also exhibited some
characteristic limitations:

(a) inflexibility in many of the major manufacturing areas, within
the service sectors and particularly in much of the public
sector. Although a great deal has changed within British industry over the last few years, there continues to be a great deal to
be done: the 1986 Incomes Data Services study on *Flexibility
at Work*² commented: 'With very few exceptions the process of
achieving full scale flexibility has hardly begun.' This inflexibility has directly affected attitudes towards quality, primarily
because each person has been able to argue that it is someone
else's responsibility. Again in the TUC guidelines on quality
circles it is interesting to note the following comment: 'Trade
unions will be particularly concerned about the employment
implications of QCs, on, for example, staff in quality control
departments as well as employees in other jobs affected by
review of work methods.' A recipe for continued inflexibility!

(b) low productivity – a great deal has been written about productivity comparisons between the UK and the rest of the
world, much of it ignoring the quality aspect of low productivity. It was interesting to compare the final assembly line at
Nissan ZAMA plant in Japan with similar plants in the UK
and the USA. It was clear, and this was confirmed by the
Japanese, that the pace of the belt was in fact *slower* than that
in the USA or UK. The explanation is the principle of 'getting
it right first time' – if this meant that the belt should travel
slower to ensure that quality standards were at the highest
level, then in the end the productivity gain was far greater. If
there is a difference between the Japanese and the British
worker, it is that the Japanese worker works at a steady
medium pace through all the shift, whereas the British worker
tends to work more variably – which in the end results in lower
quality standards and lower productivity levels

(c) a belief that quality is someone else's job – much of this
attitude has arisen from a high level of inspection procedures.
Successful quality programmes are based on *self*-inspection
and a personal commitment to the highest quality standards.
This cannot be achieved with high levels of inspection which,
despite changes in recent years, remain characteristic of many
parts of British industry and commerce.

British industry and commerce is saddled with many unhealthy legacies from the past. Important changes *have* taken place (see Chapter 5), but the challenge of Japan and Europe still needs to be faced head-on. The second part of this book will consider the way ahead.

Chapter 4
THE JAPANESE INFLUENCE: MYTH OR REALITY?

The Japanese influence on total quality appears to be very considerable. Much of the early success by Deming in influencing thinking on total quality was done within the Japanese context. I have also made reference to a number of specific Japanese experiences which indicate their approach to total quality. The Japanese have achieved phenomenal success throughout the world in persuading customers that all their goods and services are produced to the highest quality standards. At the same time, there has been a tendency for Western management to assume that, however great the Japanese influence on total quality, it is something peculiarly Japanese and related to cultural and other factors which cannot be translated into the Western context. In understanding the Japanese approach to total quality, an understanding of their management and business philosophy is essential. In a notable series of seven articles in the *Financial Times* as long ago as 1981, Christopher Lorenz commented:

> Despite all the current western alarms about robot factories, the consistent theme behind Japan's rise to industrial pre-eminence has not until recently been due to particularly advanced technology, certainly not in product design. Instead the key has been the efficient, reliable improvement and manufacture of relatively standard designs. Central to that approach has been a universal commitment to quality within the country's leading companies from the very top to the bottom of the enterprise.

A look at management and business philosophy within Japan finds the Japanese businessman primarily concerned with growth inside his (or her) particular business sector. Obviously profitability is important, because it is accepted that no company can operate indefinitely at a loss, but profitability is not the only yardstick of achievement. The security and growth of the company are considered just as important. While efficiency is a key factor for Western management, permanency plays a similar role in Japan.

The emphasis, therefore, is on long-term growth and development by innovation and diversification. The priority is long-term profits, instead of allowing short-term profit considerations to influence decision making. As a result, the installation of new technology in the form of more automation and the greater use of robots are seen as inevitable trends in manufacture, though management consider it essential to install new plant in order to seek continuous improvement and achieve the highest quality standards.

This emphasis on long-term growth and permanence as a business philosophy has a major influence on the management style within Japanese industry and commerce. Underlying this approach is the lifetime employment system, which emphasizes the long-term interdependence of company and employee. The strength of this system was recently summarized by the president of the Sony corporation: 'Fortunately Japan has a lifetime employment system which encourages a long-range view even among lower and middle management levels.' This also means that top management are usually thoroughly familiar with their organization, having worked their way through the system. Furthermore, there is emphasis on non-specialization, whereby employees (particularly those likely to move through to management) are rotated through all the functions. A good example of this was at Canon: I found a young graduate who was destined for the commercial function working full time for two years on the production line – being rotated and moving around the departments – to familiarize himself with the technology before he was expected to sell it.

This practice at Canon also reflects the considerable emphasis on training and development. The security of long-term employment and constant on-the-job training are certainly among the major reasons for Japan's high commitment among its workforce to total quality and continuous improvement. With this emphasis on the longer term, 'bottom up' decision making is particularly strong, because there is less emphasis on top management 'leading from the front'. As a result, the Japanese view is very much that everybody within the organization is responsible for improving quality;

investment in people, therefore, will pay major dividends in quality improvement. This approach is complemented by decision making being devolved to the lowest practicable level; reference is only made to higher authority when absolutely necessary while most decisions are taken at the bottom level. This style is a key to understanding the high level of involvement and commitment of employees to a total quality programme. It is also important to recognize that it has some obvious defects: it often takes up a great deal of time, it is ill-fitted to cope with crises and can lead to homogenized compromise decisions.

Nevertheless, it is in this environment of long-term management thinking and commitment to involving people that the development of total quality has been achieved in Japan. In particular, it has created an environment where attitudes often prevalent in the UK in the past – distrust, resistance to change and conflict – are much less apparent in Japan.

Against this background, it is interesting to see how Japanese management look at the approach to total quality within their organizations. They start by indicating that top management are responsible for laying down objectives in the form of policy and strategy. Middle management are responsible for identifying the problems which are important for the best results and require urgent attention, considering how solutions can be identified and organizing the workforce to look for such solutions. At the third level, the emphasis is on actually solving working-level problems. This can be illustrated in the diagram (see Figure 5). The influence of Juran on this is quite apparent.

With this general approach, the Japanese over the last 25 years have moved from company-wide quality control within the manufacturing industry to quality control for subcontractors and suppliers in the late 60s and early 70s; to non-manufacturing industries, such as construction, by the mid-70s; and since that time into the service industries, such as banking, hotels and restaurants. The total quality approach now applies to every type of job in every kind of industry. Today, according to JUSE's Junji Noguchi, quality control in Japan has six principal features:

- company-wide quality control – all parts of an organization co-operate to improve quality, which has been broadened to incorporate *all* aspects of company operations, including

Figure 5   QC Activities at Different Levels

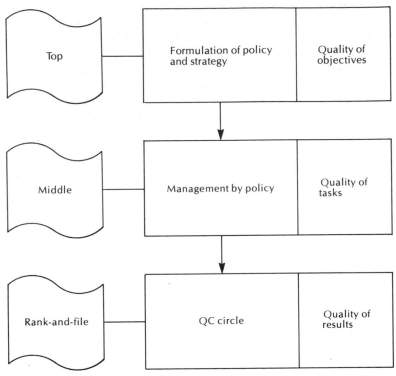

| Top | Formulation of policy and strategy | Quality of objectives |

| Middle | Management by policy | Quality of tasks |

| Rank-and-file | QC circle | Quality of results |

Source: *Dentsu Japan Marketing/Advertising,* Autumn 1984[1]

productivity, efficiency and energy savings. Assistance is often given to company suppliers to achieve the necessary quality standards. It is interesting to note that a lot of the suppliers of major motor manufacturers – such as Toyota and Nissan – are in fact single suppliers and are often wholly owned by the main organization as part of its method of ensuring the highest quality standards.

● quality control audits – whereby top management examine the quality effectiveness, not only within an organization, but also within subsidiaries and suppliers

● education and training – whereby most major organizations hold regular training sessions on all aspects of quality from

board level down to the lowest level, with particular emphasis on understanding statistical techniques
- quality circles – which underpin all total quality programmes and provide the main thrust for problem solving
- application of statistical methods – where a set of common statistical tools are used as a common language at all levels. Many of these techniques are learnt at school
- nationwide quality activities – there are annual, regional and national conferences held for management and employees so that quality issues common to one or more industries can be explored and solutions found

The emphasis in Japan is always on the long term. It is interesting to read an article[1] by the president of a major service organization, Yoshinobu Hattori, which particularly emphasizes that:

> It takes at least four or five years to introduce and establish TQC in a company. Thus the deciding factors are firm determination and correct understanding on the part of top management rather than favourable conditions.

This is an attitude which would raise many eyebrows among Western managers.

A number of key characteristics seem to dominate the Japanese approach to management, which in turn flows into their approach to total quality. There is, nevertheless, nothing dramatic or new about their approach, just a systematic and dedicated long-term philosophy. As one might expect, the Japanese approach largely reflects the early messages provided by Deming, which they have consolidated and built into their particular culture.

The Japanese way is not unique. Japanese management have made total quality work by using simple techniques and involving everybody within the organization in applying those techniques, emphasizing continuous improvement and total quality. There is nothing in their approach that suggests it cannot be adopted and adapted to meet needs within the UK environment. The reality is that it *could* work within the UK, it is a myth that it is simply not transferable.

Within the UK, a significant number of major Japanese companies have shown that it is possible, while taking account of the culture and management style of the UK, to bring the Japanese approach into the UK environment. YKK, the zip manufacturers, were one of the first to move into the UK, in the North West. Visiting the factory shortly after returning from Japan, it was apparent to me that they had harnessed the energies and commitment of the workforce in much the same way. Quality standards were paramount, with high visibility of senior management (who included Japanese) within the overall environment. Sony (Bridgend) provided another relatively early model and, more recently, the experiences of Toshiba and Nissan have shown that it is possible to adapt the Japanese approach to the UK environment. In all cases, much of the management was British. It is interesting to note Peter Wickens's comment in *The Road to Nissan*:[2].

> In summary, quality of work will only be high if the individual is fully motivated. While we may say that quality must be 'built into' the job this will only happen if the right attitude to quality comes from within the individual. No amount of exhortation will achieve genuine commitment to quality – wall posters and slogans will fail. It is a key management responsibility and can be obtained only if we realize that it is total motivation that matters.

This approach, as used in the UK, reflects the underlying approach in Japan and demonstrates clearly the possibility of transferring, with appropriate adjustments, the Japanese total quality approach to the UK environment. What is perhaps of more concern is the Japanese answer when they were asked why Japanese companies in Japan had thrown open their factories, talked frankly to members of the Pacific Basin Study Mission in 1984 about their techniques and shown them the secrets of their success; the reply was: 'Because it would take you ten years to get to where we are now – and by that time we shall be further ahead. And besides we know you won't do it!' The reality of Japanese influence lies in that very challenge.

Chapter 5
EUROPEAN COMPARISONS

In 1989, two years after the first European congress on quality circles and management, a second congress took place in Strasbourg. Europe in 1989 is much concerned with the prospect of the single European market due to come into operation in 1992. Within this context, total quality is perceived as central to the performance of European industry and commerce, and it is clear that a number of Europe-wide initiatives are under way in order to protect the European market against fierce Japanese and US competition and to strengthen the European position in international markets.

Against this background, total quality is a theme which is beginning to have a major impact across the whole of Europe in all sectors of the economy. It is characterized by:

● pan-European co-operation on major projects (as in the aerospace industry), based on shared values about quality standards
● a major drive to introduce Europe-wide certification standards which will apply throughout Europe after 1992
● the establishment of a European quality management foundation (initially funded by 14 major multinational corporations such as Philips, Volkswagen and British Telecom) with the aim of creating a positive quality image
● the introduction of quality issues into schools and other educational establishments, both in teaching techniques and by actually involving groups in problem-solving something which has long existed within Japan
● a particular emphasis on introducing total quality through participative management on the basis that quality cannot be achieved without participation, without dialogue, without listening to clients and one's fellow workers – a theme less emphasized in the UK environment

- a major extension of the total quality approach into service industries, with the airlines, hotels and financial services particularly prominent
- a marked growth in the application of total quality programmes to small or medium-sized organizations, often driven by the demands of their customers (who, as in Japan, are sometimes large corporations keen to reduce their inventories)
- an extension of the idea of total quality, within the manufacturing sector (and particularly the major organizations), beyond the direct production areas and into, for example, the staff and administrative functions
- major developments in the public sector (although there is still a long way to go), including airport authorities in Portugal, the telephone service, social security offices and postal services in France, housing associations and the national labour market board (the same as our Job Centres in the UK) in Sweden, all motivated to a large extent by the drive to improve the effectiveness and efficiency of public services. There is a growing recognition that the concept of quality needs to be defined, not specifically as conforming to customer requirements but as providing a cost-effective service to people who often do not have a choice about whether they use the service or not.

The national labour market board in Sweden shows how the concept of total quality can be applied in a public service organization. The stress is always on achieving real results and motivating staff to improve the quality of service. It also integrates the value system of the different sectors of the economy in order to generate commitment and results. Thus, the ideals of public administration (justice, legality, security and openness), business (goals, efficiency and results) and the popular movement (commitment to common goals) are all combined. The many other examples within Europe of introducing total quality to the public service show that one of the keys to success is measuring existing performance and customer requirements in real terms, however one defines the customer. The approach has harnessed the energies of people, in a way not normally associated with such organizations, to achieve real results.

The other fundamental characteristic which has been emerging in Europe during 1989 is the recognition that the introduction of total quality on a Europe-wide basis is an extremely long-term strategy. As an example, Philips (the electrical giant) have identified seven steps in achieving total quality:

Step 1 – conventional quality approach
Step 2 – introduction of company-wide quality initiative (CWQI)
Step 3 – process control
Step 4 – process improvement
Step 5 – CWQI breakthrough
Step 6 – strategic breakthrough
Step 7 – excellence.

The company claims that it has now completed the first three steps, which has taken some *five years*. Achievement of excellence will take a total of *20 years*, as in the long-term Japanese approach which has proved so successful. Philips have also identified a number of crucial stages:

● awareness and commitment – the process by which the company thoroughly investigates all aspects of quality (including competition and customer requirements) and generates the highest level of commitment to the new approach
● organization and planning: the company prepares in detail the CWQI
● implementation, which only commences once thorough preparation has been carried out
● monitoring and recognition whereby the actual improvements generated by the programme are carefully monitored and the company ensures that success is properly recognized
● renewal: CWQI is a learning process and there is no ideal approach, so there is emphasis on continuous innovation and the development of professionalism throughout the company in terms of total quality.

The Philips approach to CWQI is based on:

● the top-down cascade whereby top management clearly drives the whole programme
● management ownership at all levels, whereby it is recognized that line management must have prime responsibility for quality

- involvement of all levels within the organization, based on the company-wide philosophy
- consistent behaviour (very reminiscent of the Japanese approach) which takes a particular theme and consistently manages it long term to achieve success
- a step-by-step approach to breakthrough based on the Deming principle of continuous improvement which emphasizes that the small steps are as important as the major steps in achieving breakthrough
- market-performance evidence, since good quality performance can only be related back to the marketplace
- no reliance on a simple (or simplistic) recipe – a recognition that there is no single approach to total quality and that each organization and subsidiary within Philips must develop its own particular solutions to the overall CWQI.

In the early 1980s, there was some evidence to suggest that Europe generally had been slow to respond to some of the pressures created by the Japanese in total quality. By 1989 it is apparent that total quality is as much a part of good management practice within Europe as within the UK. With the increasing competition likely to result from the effects of 1992, it is likely that the trends within Europe outlined above will develop into a significant factor in the competitiveness of European organizations. More important, the UK will have to respond to these developments even more positively in all sectors of the economy if it is to remain competitive in 1992.

Chapter 6
SOME POSITIVE INITIATIVES

The crucial problem within British industry and commerce is a problem of attitudes and ways of behaving rather than a churlish resistance to the introduction of higher quality standards. In recognition of this, the 1982 government white paper 'Standards, Quality and International Competitiveness' emphasized the government's view that quality, standards, design, marketing and delivery are all inseparable parts of a single whole which, as the performance of many of the UK's international competitors has shown, is essential to maintaining and enhancing our competitive position.[1] The white paper identified four broad areas in which government could help increase the efficiency of industry and commerce by promoting the importance of quality and encouraging the use of standards:

(a) government encouragement of certification schemes, the development of a national accreditation system and a recognizable accreditation mark, and the launch of a quality awareness campaign
(b) co-operation between government and the British Standards Institution to develop appropriate up-to-date standards which could be used by industry and commerce to enhance their position both at home and abroad
(c) a greater commitment by government to use standards as far as possible when drawing up regulations (for instance, in the areas of consumer safety and health and safety at work)
(d) greater effort by public purchasers to examine how far products built to existing standards could fulfil their requirements as effectively as their own specifications.

Considerable progress has been made since the introduction of the white paper, which was followed by the National Quality Campaign, a major government initiative to raise awareness of the importance of quality and, more specifically, British Standard

5750. These government initiatives recognized the need for a major national approach to improving quality standards and enhancing management's efforts.

The National Quality Campaign was launched in 1983 in order to publicize and promote a 'company-wide' commitment to quality involving all levels from top management down. The idea was to make everybody aware of the importance of their own particular role and how it can contribute to improvements in total quality. The campaign included the production of a wide range of written and other material, a high-level study trip to the Pacific Basin, the introduction of British quality awards and a major advertising campaign. As the ODI survey has demonstrated, awareness was certainly increased, but the action level still leaves much to be desired.

BS5750

The BS5750 series provides the national standards which tell suppliers and manufacturers what is required of a quality system. They look at quality in the sense of fitness and safety in use: in other words, is the service provided or the product designed and constructed to satisfy the customer's needs? It is the British Standard which was adopted as the International Standard for Quality Systems known as ISO 9000.

BS5750 lays down the requirements for a cost-effective quality management system and provides a structured approach on which to base that system. It is not a product standard or specification and does not attempt to establish a level of quality for a product. The requirements included in the standard allow a system to be developed around established guidelines which are known to have been effective in other organizations. Regardless of the industry concerned or the numbers employed, the principles remain valid. The ways of achieving them may differ and each industry will tend to have its own way of expressing its requirements, but the underlying objectives are the same. In short, BS5750 sets out how an organization can establish, document and maintain an effective quality system which will demonstrate to customers that the organization is committed to quality and is able to meet their quality needs. Specific requirements include:

(a) a senior manager with the necessary authority must clearly be responsible for quality, with the task of co-ordinating and monitoring the quality system and seeing that prompt and effective action is taken to ensure that the requirements of BS 5750 are met

(b) the nature and degree of organization, structure, resources, responsibilities, procedures and processes affecting quality must be documented

(c) the quality system must be planned and developed to take account of all other functions such as customer liaison, manufacturing, purchasing, subcontracting, training and installation

(d) quality planning must identify the need for updating quality control techniques, ensuring there are equipment and personnel capable of carrying out plans and providing for adequate quality records

(e) there must be carefully planned and documented control of design and development planning, with assignment of activities to qualified staff with adequate resources, control of interfaces between different disciplines and organizations, documentation of design input requirements and design output

(f) the establishment of a co-ordinated system that will ensure that all appropriate documents covering planning, design, packaging, manufacture and inspection of product as well as procedures which describe how functions shall be controlled, who is in control, what is to be controlled, where and when

(g) control in writing of purchased product and services, purchasing data, inspection and verification of purchased product and the quality system to be applied (as appropriate) by the suppliers

(h) the establishment of procedures and work instructions, including all customer specifications, in a simple form which covers every phase of manufacture, assembly and installation

(i) procedures for inspection and tests to be performed on incoming goods, taking account of the documented evidence of conformance provided with the goods

(j) procedures and records covering the control, calibration and inspection of measuring and test equipment

(k) written control procedures in order to establish quickly at all times whether product has:

- not been inspected
- been inspected and approved
- been inspected and rejected

(l) systems for prompt and effective corrective action where non-conformance has been found

(m) written instructions and procedures on the way product is handled, stored and protected in the process and as it moves through the plant

(n) detailed records that customer quality requirements are being met, including data such as audit reports on the quality assurance system, results of inspections and tests, calibration of test and measuring equipment and corrective action

(o) effective internal quality audit systems monitored by management

(p) provision of training, and records of training and achievements of competence

(q) clear statistical procedures for monitoring quality standards.

By following the guidelines set out above, organizations can then approach an appropriate certification body in order to achieve accreditation, which demonstrates their adherence to the appropriate quality standards.

BS 5750 provides a framework for management action in establishing quality standards. It is not a recipe for total quality management since it does not in itself gain the commitment of everybody in an organization to a total quality programme. There are now some 9,000 firms assessed and registered by second and third parties against BS 5750 or directly equivalent standards. This has provided a framework, in large sectors of British industry and commerce, for helping to build up confidence in the standards and quality of British goods and services both in the UK and abroad. It also forms the basis for the development of total quality campaigns and programmes within individual organizations.

There is little doubt that attitudes are beginning to change to quality and quality standards. Certainly the level of awareness has been greatly increased by the success stories – Jaguar, British Airways, Black and Decker, Rank Xerox, Wedgwood and, more recently, British Steel – where improvements in business performance have been achieved through commitment to total quality. Nevertheless, as I have already indicated, survival in a world of global competition and a single European Market requires more than a shift in attitudes in a few major organizations. It requires a wholesale adoption of the principles and practices of total quality throughout *all* sectors of the UK economy, including the public sector. There still remains a great deal to be done.

Chapter 7
CONCLUSIONS AND LESSONS

In the previous chapters I have considered some of the key international influences on the total quality movement and then examined some of the developments in Japan, Europe and within the UK. In endeavouring to provide a basic understanding of quality and how different organizations approach it within their own national boundaries, I have tried to create a framework of understanding. A number of general conclusions and some specific lessons can be identified from this process.

General conclusions

There are probably three major general conclusions that can be identified and form the basis for understanding quality and how it can be applied within organizations. These are considered below.

Common themes

In reviewing thirty years of quality management, it is apparent to me that there are some common themes which run through all the key influences. These are considered in more detail under the specific lessons below, but enough evidence has now accumulated to show that there is nothing special or magical about total quality and quality management. While there are differences in emphasis and phraseology, there is ultimately a common approach throughout the world.

Japan – nothing special

A great deal has been written about Japanese methods and their contribution to quality management over the last thirty years.

Clearly there are cultural differences between Japan and the Western world, but the very fact that a Western academic, Deming, had such a profound influence on Japanese thinking is an indication that there is nothing special or unique about the Japanese character that makes them able to apply total quality in a different way from the West. In simple terms, the Japanese style of management, with its 'bottom up' decision-making process, openness about information and long-term investment in people, has inevitably created an environment in which attitudes so prevalent in the UK industry – distrust, resistance to change and inflexibility – are much less apparent. This approach, however, is not at all revolutionary. It implies only that people can work for the common goal of total quality, that commitment to this goal can be developed, that to achieve this commitment there must be proper investment in training and development, that achievements are properly recognized, that decision making is decentralized to the lowest possible level wherever possible and that achieving the highest quality standards is a co-operative effort involving all employees at all levels. These are the ways in which the best organizations in the West have always motivated their managers. The Japanese have successfully extended the same principles to the whole workforce – and surely *that* is the basis of how the Japanese success in achieving the highest quality standards can be adapted to the UK environment.

A world-wide phenomenon

While I have not considered in detail the total quality approach throughout the world, I have nevertheless emphasized some key influences which are beginning to take root not only in Japan but also in Europe and, of course, the United States and many other developed and developing countries. I was interested to see in a National Quality Campaign booklet a reference to the so-called quality jungle:

> On the general problem of terminology, the Tanzanian observers indicated that they were not only confused by the problem of levels, categories and tiers, but also by the use of terms such as QA (quality assurance), QC (quality control), quality system, quality programme, quality plan and quality verification.[1]

This is taken from the minutes of a meeting of the International Standards Organisation Committee on Quality Systems in Paris in 1982 and reflected the fact that quality is now an issue for all countries, developed and developing. The message to the UK is that we cannot afford, in the current highly competitive environment, to do anything but respond to the world-wide total quality movement based on ensuring that organizations at all times aim to meet the quality standards set by the customers. The alternative is summed up by one of the adverts in the National Quality Campaign: 'Any last requests before the quality of the competition kills your business?'

Specific lessons

In reviewing developments in the quality field a number of specific lessons can also be drawn.

Attitudes

Achieving quality standards within organizations is about attitudes at all levels. Quality is *not* just about systems, is not just about using specific techniques and tools or complying with BS 5750. Quality is about the attitude of mind of all the individuals within organizations, it is about winning the hearts and minds not only of them but also of customers who must come to believe that the organization produces goods or services which meet their specific requirements. Creating an environment and implementing a programme which recognizes the crucial importance of attitudes in an organization is the key to the long-term success and profitability of that organization.

Management

Management has the key responsibility in any total quality programme. I have often been amazed how this obvious point is only paid lip service in many organizations. I have often presented to both top and middle management the basic prerequisites of any total quality programme and started with the need for top management commitment and middle management involvement. Sage heads have nodded round the table in acknowledging and agreeing with this approach. The fact that they have agreed with the principle has often been interpreted as the beginning and end of their commitment! As the Japanese have indicated, management responsibility is absolute, a part of the overall process in the same way that meeting targets is. Juran indicated that it is essential that management is provided with the opportunity to break out of the vicious circle of.endless firefighting so as to respond and plan for the future in a total quality programme.

Involvement

Quality involves everybody within an organization. It is not the specific responsibility of any particular individual or group of individuals. Again in the National Quality Campaign, two particular advertisements reflected the importance of this aspect: 'Quality is too important to leave to your quality controllers' and 'Why should he [meaning the shop floor worker] care about quality if you [the manager] don't?'

Crosby, Juran and Deming have all emphasized this particular point and the Japanese have demonstrated in practice how it can be achieved. Again lip service is often paid within the UK to this concept, yet in many organizations different groups are either left out or allowed to opt out. The European experience of total quality, particularly in France, indicates the importance of involving everybody in a highly participative approach. This does not confirm all the usual fears one finds in the UK of 'management losing control'. It is about involvement, about recognizing that *everybody* has a contribution to make to total quality. It is also about teamwork and common goals which integrate different parts of organizations into a whole. As I have already indicated, one of the classic difficulties I come across in British industry is the 'them and us' divisions between production and engineering, and also between the different engineering factions. Too often engineering regard quality as essentially a production matter and can only respond to short-term emergencies. Even where planned maintenance programmes exist, they do not have, and are not seen to have, a role in any total quality programme without a major effort in integrating them into a whole.

Continuous improvement

Long-term continuous improvement is emphasized particularly by Deming and again demonstrated so clearly by the Japanese. Western management has not always been good at adopting particular approaches on a long-term basis. Too often one hears comments about 'flavours of the month' made cynically, especially by the shop floor and middle management. Who can blame them? Over the years we have had so many fads and techniques which have come and gone. The Japanese have demonstrated so potently (and at the cost of major industries) how a steady commitment to continuous improvement and total quality can revolutionize industry and bring enhanced competitiveness and profitability in the long term.

Training and development

Training and development play a key role at all levels in the organization and this should be continuous. In helping organizations to implement total quality programmes, training has certainly been regarded as something for the shop floor and supervision, probably for middle management, but only minimally for top management. It has taken some considerable effort to ensure that *all* levels understand not only the programme as a whole but the various techniques and tools associated with the programme. Otherwise defensiveness can creep in if the lower levels seem more knowledgeable about such things. Investment in training is a critical factor in the success of a total quality programme; it requires all levels to be involved and to attend, compulsorily, without excuse.

PART II

Implementing a Total Quality Programme

PART II

Implementing a Total
Quality Programme

Chapter 8
THE BASIC PRINCIPLES

A successful total quality programme must be based on certain basic principles. I will now consider in detail how to approach its implementation. Underlying the whole approach are six fundamental requirements, based on the concept that people are at the heart of a successful programme. These are:

- top management commitment
- attitude change
- continuous improvement
- strengthened supervision
- extensive training
- recognition of performance.

These are considered in detail below.

Top management commitment

Top management should continuously reinforce a total quality programme by what they do. Whether in management meetings, company magazines or newsletters, they should ensure their complete commitment to the approach. Despite the fact that key influences on the quality movement have emphasized the importance of management commitment since the late 1950s, the disturbing thing is we still do not seem in general to have made the breakthrough in Western management. In Japan, and increasingly in the Pacific basin, no member of management can have any doubts about the need for his or her complete commitment to the total quality process.

British shortcomings in this respect can often be explained through short-term perspectives by management, pressures to achieve short-term results and concern about costs. We have to recognize that changing management attitudes is the key to success within an organization – and that must start at the very top. In one major seafood organization, at the start of a total quality programme, the site director (who was a main board director) told his middle management that there could be no doubt of the importance of quality in maintaining the organization's leading position in the marketplace and that the purpose of the total quality programme was to ensure it. In introducing me he made it clear that he would consider it quite unacceptable if I reported that his management was not *positively* supporting the programme. The future success of the organization was dependent on his commitment and their commitment. He personally demonstrated his commitment by being highly visible in the total quality programme and thus created an environment where management knew that their performance was measured directly in their commitment and support for the programme.

To show commitment, top management should make sure that everybody within the organization from top to bottom is clear about the long-term goals – this affects management style, the quality of communications, indeed *everything* that is done within an organization.

Attitude change

Total quality requires a complete change in the attitude and culture prevailing within organizations. The remarkable turnround stories of Jaguar Cars and British Airways are examples where the organizations moved decisively away from a general view that delays, mistakes, defective materials were 'just part of life'. Another interesting example is SAS, the Scandinavian airline, which some years ago was losing money and drifting hopelessly in the marketplace. With a new chief executive, Jan Carlzon, the airline embarked on a major programme based on an identified market niche: the business market. The airline carried out extensive surveys of businessmen, asking what were the main factors that persuaded them to travel on a particular airline. The airline was thus able to make significant operational changes which in turn created an environment for greatly improved performance that was welcomed by the customers. Today the airline is successfully known as 'the businessman's airline'.

During the introduction of quality programmes in many different organizations and industries, the issue of attitudes has always emerged early in the process. Ask the production employees what their biggest problem is and they will almost invariably say that the machine or equipment is always breaking down. The engineers do not know how to maintain the equipment properly, they are never available and they seem to take a long time to repair breakdowns. Ask the maintenance employees what their biggest problem is and they well tell you the production workers: they never look after the equipment, they drive the equipment too hard and beyond specifications, and they will never call us out until a breakdown occurs.

Within a major seafood organization we were able to break down some of these barriers by creating much closer links between a specific engineer and a production area, so there was a mutual interest in keeping the machines going. Similar problems existed in the steel industry between production departments. Quality problems within rolling mills would almost invariably be blamed on the steel-making department, who allegedly did not produce the hot metal to specifications. Similarly you could guarantee that within the steel plant the major problems would always be referred to the blast furnace.

Some of the problems of attitude were well illustrated by the managing director of Matsushita Communication Industrial Company, Hajima Karatsu, who was summarizing the differences between what the Japanese have achieved in adopting Deming's approach and Western management:

> In Western business the super-elite give full play to their originality, but workers at the lower level are simply made to do standardized work on the basis of manuals. Originally quality control was designed to restrict the occurrence of inferior products within a certain tolerance range. In Japan, however, it has been changed into a movement for total elimination of inferior products through creative co-operation by all quarters concerned. When inferior goods are produced Japanese workers consider it a shame and even weep. Total quality control has revived an old spirit of craftsmanship at modern factories.

Achieving this type of attitude change is critical to the long-term success of a total quality programme.

Continuous improvement

Linked to attitude change is the need to create a climate of continuous improvement. Organizations need to ensure that they have real evidence at all times, through the use of statistical process control and control charts and many other simple techniques, that they understand what is happening in a particular process. This moves the culture of the organization away from checking whether a particular product or process is working effectively after the event to ensuring that one understands and identifies any quality problems early in the process and seeks continuously to improve performance. It also requires all levels to understand their responsibility for this quality process.

The most notable example that I have come across in recent years was within one of the Canon Cameras factories in Japan. It became apparent as I walked round the factory that there was no obvious inspection process. I discussed this with my hosts and found that some 10 years earlier they had had inspectors at all the major points on the assembly line checking the work that had been completed. They had slowly created an environment whereby employees and supervisors felt responsible for the quality of their areas until they reached a point where they had sufficient confidence in the process and the only formal inspection process was sample inspecting of finished cameras at the end of the production line. Bearing in mind the accepted quality of Canon cameras throughout the world, I was struck by the confidence management must have had in all concerned to allow such a situation to develop.

Traditionally the issues of quality and inspection have been confined to manufacturing processes within organizations, but for long-term success the attitude of continuous improvement should apply to *all* levels from top management downwards and to *all* parts of the process, including the offices, sales force and finance department. Whenever I go into an organization to discuss a total quality programme, I am often met with amazement, particularly in manufacturing organizations, when I suggest to top (or even middle) management that the programme should involve not only the 'shop floor' workers but also the 'white collar' employees. Not only does this attitude reflect a 'them and us' culture but it demonstrates a lack of understanding of just how inefficient an organization can be away from the direct manufacturing processes. As a small example, a secretarial quality circle group within one organization identified savings of two person years if members of staff providing material for typing (either audio or written) presented this material properly, without repeated redrafting. This represented a saving of some 9% of the total secretarial workforce.

Quality improvement should always be at the forefront of *everything* that is done, continuously reinforced and developed by management through the systems, processes and organizations which make such improvements possible. Within the steel industry in Japan it is interesting that, since the introduction of quality improvement programmes some 25 years ago, many different emphases have been placed on different aspects of the process. In the sixties the emphasis was very much on quality of product. As the oil crisis hit Japan, the emphasis changed in the early seventies to energy conservation – a major issue in the steel industry, which is a very heavy user of energy and can be badly affected by large increases in energy costs. In the late seventies and early eighties the emphasis changed again to cost and productivity; certainly by the mid eighties, when I visited the Nippon steel works, everybody was wearing CAP badges. This approach pervaded the organization and created an atmosphere whereby production and service departments worked closely together in a company-wide quality improvement programme.

At a more trivial level, a major chemical works in the North West of England set up project teams for a quality improvement programme who required specialist advice from a number of central departments. These project teams soon ground to a halt because the central departments did not consider attendance at appropriate meetings to be a priority and failed to turn up on many occasions. Breakthroughs can only be achieved by creating an environment where the organization culture allows and encourages support between different areas.

Any total quality programme is unlikely to be completely successful all of the time. Management must recognize that achieving breakthrough requires constant support and positive feedback to everyone involved. The Japanese are particularly successful at creating this environment. At Canon Cameras, I noticed lists of names indicating some sort of performance level. I was surprised at this, thinking it might be some sort of bonus system, but found it was a record of suggestions made by employees within a particular department. Any suggestion, however small, was recorded on the chart and at the end of the year there were prizes for those who had put forward the most suggestions. While the specific approach might not be appropriate to the UK environment, the underlying message was clear enough: every step needs to be taken to encourage individuals within an organization to be part of the improvement process and to look for opportunities to make changes.

Supervision

Within large parts of British industry supervision traditionally has been seen as the 'authority' within a particular department, responsible for telling the workforce what to do and taking appropriate disciplinary action if they did not comply. More recently, supervision became associated with progress chasing or, to put it another way, trying to make sure that others were doing their job properly so as to enable their department to function effectively.

The successful introduction of total quality gives a key role to supervision in ensuring that the quality message is carried down to grass-roots level. In *The Road to Nissan*, Peter Wickens shows the way forward:

> In order to enhance the responsibility and role of production supervision it is essential to give back many of the responsibilities that have been taken away over the years. Nissan supervisors are responsible for making the decisions on who will work for them; they have full responsibility for quality, housekeeping and much maintenance. Within obvious constraints they lay out their work area and material arrives blindside where *they* want it to come.

Training

If the key to success lies with supervision, then it is important to ensure that the selection, training and motivation of supervision allows for the development of the skills which enable them to become a dynamic force for improving performance. Top management needs to provide opportunities and the investment in training to ensure the quality of supervision improves. The success of a total quality programme depends on supervision (and indeed everybody!) being given the tools, skills and ability to manage the process. Too often top management confuses briefing with providing development and training. In the initial stages of any total quality programmes I have found resistance to taking supervisors away from their jobs for any length of time on the grounds that they are too busy; 'Just tell them what they need to know' is often heard. Attitude change can only be achieved through a much longer-term perspective.

One of the major successes of the Japanese approach has been the very extensive training programmes that have been used in the total quality programmes. It is interesting to note that Professor Ishikawa, often known as the 'father of quality circles', recognized in 1963 that once the extensive training of supervisors had taken place, the next logical step was to involve the shop floor. Thus were born quality circles.

> I first considered how best to get grass-roots workers to understand and practise QC (Quality control). The ideal was to educate all people working at factories throughout the country but this was asking too much. Therefore I thought of educating factory foremen or on the spot leaders in the first place.

The success of the Japanese approach to quality has been that, from the very beginning, management and supervision fully understood each step of the programme, including all the techniques and processes required.

Recognition

Motivation theory and practice emphasize strongly the importance of recognizing performance and achievement. This applies in any total quality programme, the question is how it is best achieved. The traditional suggestion scheme approach, whereby there is the link between the reward and suggestion, generally does not work in a total quality programme if ony because it creates a further layer of bureaucracy in evaluating each proposal. In Japan recognition is generally given through prizes and competitions for either the most or the 'best' proposals and projects. On a more spectacular basis, Sony selects the 'best' quality circle projects that have been carried out in all the major countries where Sony has a presence. The quality circle leaders and members meet once a year for a major quality circle convention in Tokyo, where a further competition takes place to establish the outstanding project for the year. The emphasis is very much on recognition of contribution and achievement, with no direct monetary reward.

This approach creates a momentum for the total quality programme and encourages individuals and groups to seek continuous improvement. Interestingly, the competition approach is not welcomed in all organizations: certainly in one North-Eastern-based manufacturing plant there was considerable resistance to such an approach, despite the fact that there was a successful total quality programme running. The feeling among those involved was that giving prizes could be divisive. Whatever the approach, which needs to be tailored to each organization, the key to success is that people are central to a successful total quality programme – recognizing their contribution will motivate them long term.

Chapter 9
STRATEGY DEVELOPMENT

There is nothing particularly new about a total quality programme except for the organization which is beginning to undertake such an investment. As I have demonstrated in the section 'Why Quality?', the whole issue of quality and quality improvement has existed for at least three decades and there is hard experience in Japan, Europe and the UK of successful implementation of total quality programmes. In any implementation programme one of the problems to be faced, whether as an employee advising top management in the introduction of such a programme, or as an external consultant, is that each programme has to be designed to meet the particular environment and style of an organization in a unique way. And yet the experience of many other organizations can provide a framework upon which one can build. It is important therefore, when looking at the implementation of total quality within an organization, not to ignore the advice and experiences of the key influences and the lessons from Japan and elsewhere. In particular there should be three major components of any implementation programme, as follows:

- strategy development
- planning for action
- operating elements.

This approach can be referred to as the S-P-O approach to total quality.

In my experience in helping organizations introduce total quality programmes it has become apparent that the pressure has always been to move straight to the third component, the operating elements. Organizations, and in particular top management within them, have demanded to know *how* a total quality programme could be implemented, looking at the techniques and tools available and assessing whether, as an external consultant, I was able to match their requirements. This approach greatly mirrors the style common in so many western organizations where short-term results and a tendency to adopt 'flavours of the month' have played a dominant role. Admiration of many of the Japanese results in adopting a total quality approach has often meant that western management has picked off particular techniques such as quality circles and tried to implement them in isolation from an overall company or organization policy for total quality.

Against this background, this chapter looks specifically at the strategy development phase of S-P-O. This phase is absolutely critical to the successful implementation of a total quality programme and can often last up to two years. Bearing in mind the models of Deming, Juran and others as well as the experience of the Japanese and successful companies in the West, the principal factors of any strategy aimed at the introduction of total quality should include:

● long-term approach
● integration into the management of the organization
● clearly defined focus.

Any basic management textbook will tell you that developing a management strategy of whatever kind requires as a first step understanding of the fundamental facts. Despite this, when it comes to total quality management are often looking for a quick move and implementation programme. I have often been called into organizations, as already indicated, and asked to develop within weeks if not days an implementation programme for total quality. And yet the reality, whether one looks at Japan's sustained total quality programme or even the major organizations referred to in such books as *In Search of Excellence*,[1] is that the implementation of a total quality programme is a long-term issue. No real focus to the quality programme can be given unless there is a clear understanding of three key aspects of quality within an organization as follows:

● costs – what are the real costs of quality within an organization?
● people/attitudes – what is the organizational climate?
      – how receptive or otherwise are management and work force likely to be to any major change programme?

- what are the management structures that currently exist and how flexible are they?
- what are current attitudes to customers/clients?
● what are the real customer requirements?
  - when was the last time that a market survey was carried out on customer requirements?
  - what is the market in which the organization works or delivers services?
  - is there a clear understanding of what customers/clients mean by quality?

Most organizations may be able to answer some or all of these questions in isolation but often there is no true integration of all these aspects of quality management and no proper understanding of the facts at the highest management level. The first aspect therefore of strategy development is to ensure there is a complete understanding of these three major elements.

Cost of quality

We have already defined quality as meaning 'fitness of purpose' and 'the ability to satisfy a given need'. In many organizations these definitions are measured by the direct cost of rectification or replacement to customers for faulty products or services. The reality is that quality-related costs are incurred in the design, implementation, operation and maintenance of quality management systems, plus the costs incurred owing to the failure of the systems or products. So quality related costs are not, as is sometimes thought, just the cost of quality assurance, inspection and scrap materials. They arise from a range of activities, all of which may impinge on the quality of product or service. Cullen and Hollingum[2] demonstrate clearly how manufacturing variance can be generated through every function within the organization (Figure 6).

In carrying out a diagnosis of all the costs of quality within the organization it is essential that every department is asked to carry out an analysis, focusing on two aspects:

● those aspects that affect the actual quality of the work done by the department

Figure 6 The Importance of Quality in the Different Manufacturing Functions

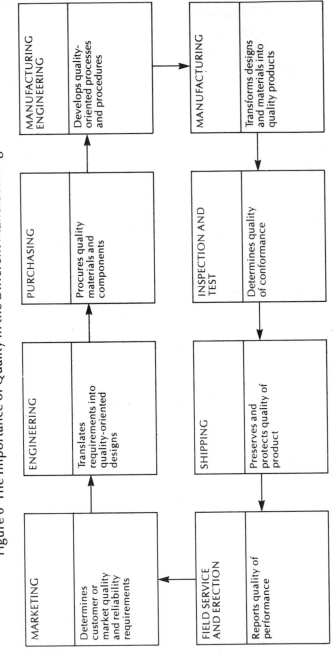

Source: Cullen and Hollingum, *Implementing Total Quality*

● those aspects that affect the quality of the work done by other departments.

This introduces for the first time into the organization the customer/supplier concept whereby each department is both a customer of another department in terms of the goods or services supplied and each department is a supplier to another department of goods and services. By adopting this approach it is possible to instill within an organization the concept of being responsible for the quality of product or service at source rather than allowing some other part of the organization to accept or reject the quality of a particular product or service. In this way an organization can establish the concept of the quality network (Figure 7).

Within this overall framework of the quality network, it is possible to consider quality costs under four main categories:

● costs of prevention
● costs of appraisal
● costs of internal failure
● costs of external failure.

These are considered in more detail below.

Costs of prevention

This covers all those factors which contribute to ensuring that the provision of goods and services achieves the relevant quality standards, in other words 'getting it right first time'. It covers the costs of design to meet the appropriate conformance standards, the overall costs of running a quality assurance system, such as that covered by BS 5750, and the introduction of a total quality programme. A simple example can be shown within a male toiletries organization where a major problem was identified in the provision of gift set samples to clients as part of the overall marketing and sales campaign. Significant efforts were made to design and introduce a detailed programme to ensure these samples were available at the appropriate time to meet customer requirements. The costs of prevention were the costs of introducing such a system, although the overall result was a significant cost saving and improvement in quality standards by proper design and planning of the system. The Japanese have shown above all else how invest-

Figure 7 The Quality Network

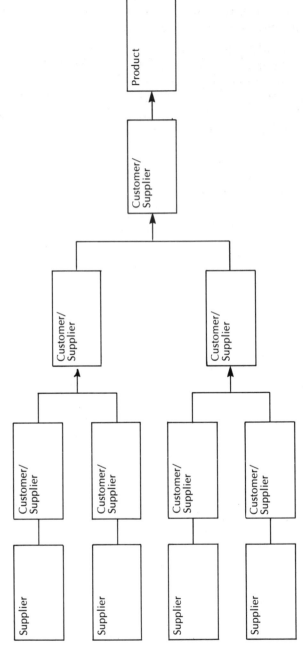

Source: Cullen and Hollingum, *Implementing Total Quality*

ment in the costs of prevention is critical to improvement of quality standards. In many cases much of the investment is difficult to measure because ultimately it reflects the introduction of systems and procedures which have a direct effect on attitudes and commitment to quality. During my visit to Canon Cameras, management had some difficulty in identifying many of the costs of prevention because they had now become part and parcel of the management system.

Costs of appraisal

These costs cover the inspection and related costs involved in ensuring the highest quality standards. Traditionally industry and commerce have had inspections at each stage of the customer/supplier network, from inspection of products being supplied into organizations to banks of inspectors at different stages in the production line. This particular cost of quality has always been the more obvious one and is easily identifiable. In the steel industry within the UK, traditionally quality was inspected by having inspectors and laboratory technicians at each stage of the process checking the quality standards, whether it be of the coke, of the iron coming out of the blast furnaces, of the steel or of the finished rolled products.The major changes within the steel industry in the UK as it has become profitable and efficient have been achieved through technology and significant changes of attitudes. This included a radical shift away from large investment in inspectors to a reduction in numbers whereby the production operatives are now responsible for the quality of the product at whatever stage. The chemical industry also invests heavily in costs of appraisal mainly through extensive laboratory testing of the product at each stage. Much of this routine testing, often away from the immediate production areas, can be made the responsibility of production with appropriately reduced costs.

Costs of internal failure

These costs refer to those associated with the reworking of a product or service as a result of a failure to meet quality standards which has been identified within the organization responsible.

These costs are often built into manufacturing costs and appear to be an accepted part of the cycle. A good example of this was within a major iron pipe making organization where, because faulty pipes could be recycled back through the melting process, there was a tendency to accept this as effectively a 'no cost' item, other than the problems associated with failure to meet production schedules. Yet the costs of this recycling process, involving the transport of a heavy pipe back to the melting plant, the reprocessing of the pipe, which may also include cutting the pipe into manageable sections, and actual cost of production up to the point where the metal was back in the pipe spinning plant, were enormous.

One interesting way of raising awareness about the costs of internal failure was demonstrated within Nissan's ZAMA plant near Tokyo. As already mentioned, reject items and problem items were put on display near the assembly line, both to demonstrate the likely quality problems but also to maintain high visibility. For instance, a problem of cracking had occurred in the rear red plastic brakelight cover. By displaying this in the area it was not only possible to identify that there was an internal failure cost, but in addition the problem – rubber trims which were slightly out of specification and too small were causing the brakelight covers to crack when being fitted – was quickly identified and resolved.

Costs of external failure

These are the costs which are incurred once product and service are delivered to customers and clients. The obvious costs include the cost of the administration service supporting warranty claims and related customer complaints and the costs of replacement and repair. Quite often these costs are considered part of 'good customer relations' and are often separated from the main production and delivery departments. For instance within a major Japanese sales and distribution arm of an electrical goods manufacturer the customer service began to grow significantly, partly as a result of company growth but partly as a result of increasing complaints and queries. The marketing department had put particular emphasis on the need to ensure that there were good customer relations by responding quickly and efficiently to all queries and complaints. It was some time before there was proper recognition, as part of a total quality programme which was being introduced, that the problem was not a matter of being able to respond to external failures, which was becoming an increasing cost, but in ensuring that the problems were prevented in the first place – ie. investing in the costs of prevention.

In addition to the obvious costs of external failure, there are some very significant hidden costs, particularly in relation to the reputation of the organization and to possible market loss. For example, the experience of the Xerox corporation prior to the introduction of their total quality programme was that the main competition, particularly the Japanese, were producing machines of comparable copy quality and comparable reliability but in many cases at less cost than Xerox. The total quality programme in Xerox was aimed among many other things at reducing some of the hidden quality costs associated with loss of market position.

The ODI survey of chief executives confirms strongly how important a reputation for quality is in the long-term survival of an organization. This reputation for quality cannot be bought with a very high investment in dealing with external failures. Organizations with the best reputations for quality have recognized the hidden costs of external failure.

In analyzing these costs, it is possible to identify two major reasons for quality problems:

- assignable causes
- random variations.

Assignable causes

These are causes of quality problems which can be directly traced and are usually due to errors of some kind. For instance, they may be due to errors in design either because a wrong decision has been made or there has been some simple error in specification, to errors in production such as operator errors or breakdowns in equipment, to errors in administration such as wrong information on invoices or misunderstandings about the invoice system, or to errors in not clearly identifying market/customer requirements and providing the wrong specification.

Some examples will help to show that it is not always easy to trace assignable causes. Within a major seafood organization a number of difficulties were being experienced by the failure of suppliers to supply on time as a result of stops being put on the organization's account through non-payment. This was initially traced to inefficiencies in the accounts department who at the end of each period were faced with major inputting and cheque run problems within a very tight timetable. The first reaction of the organization was to consider increasing the number of staff within the accounts function, but there was some resistance to this because outside end of month periods there was a certain slackness in the system. After more detailed investigation it was found that the cause of the problem was not in fact within the accounts department. The problem arose from outlying branch managers holding on to invoices from suppliers till the end of the month, when they sent them as a batch to the central accounts office. They considered they were helping the organization both in sending batches and in holding on to invoices as long as possible to improve the cashflow situation. In fact the problem was quite the reverse, affecting supplies to the organization which affected production schedules and ultimately customers. The message clearly is that the obvious assignable cause is not necessarily the only one.

Another area which causes considerable difficulty is within service industries in relation to customer requirements. It is often easy to identify that there has been a failure to meet customer requirements – because the customer has complained. The assignable cause – which is clearly failure to meet customer requirements or specifications – can be difficult to trace because within the service sector it is not always possible to identify clearly what exactly are the customer requirements. A good example of this was within an industrial catering organization with a vending operation. The vending management identified in a number of cases a customer requirement for increasing sophistication and quality in the machines to produce the highest quality coffee and related products. The more sophisticated machines needed more servicing and as a result were more prone to break down and malfunction. While this could be traced directly to a number of causes, much of the problem was a misinterpretation of customer requirements, the prime requirement being the ability to produce the products reliably on a mass basis. With the removal of the sophisticated machine and the installation of a machine which was capable of mass vending but produced a lower quality product, customer requirements were met. The initial reaction however of the vending management was to complain to the manufacturers of the equipment that it was not of a high enough standard. In fact the assignable cause was a misinterpretation of customer requirements and usage.

Random variations

These refer to causes of the problem where no pattern or set of reasons emerges to determine why variations in quality occur. While, as is clear, these causes can be random, they can to some extent be controlled. The key to controlling random variations is first eliminating all assignable causes and then trying to keep the random variations within specified parameters or controls. This can be done by using statistical techniques to monitor variations within bands of control.

An example of this was within an iron melting plant producing molten metal which was used in the production of iron pipes. Within the total quality programme it was possible over a period of time to reduce significantly assignable causes of poor yield and sub-specification molten metal by introducing more sophisticated equipment to monitor temperature within the melting plant, by controlling more closely the speed of the melting process and by more obvious measures to avoid spillages and wastage. This enabled the plant management and work force to concentrate on the random causes of yield variation: in particular the eviromental temperature, unpredictable scrap quality and unpredictable coke quality. By applying careful controls using simple statistical techniques the yield of the plant improved significantly with less random variations. The biggest breakthrough involved a myth that yield could not be improved beyond a certain level because of the unpredictable element of the processes which took place within the furnaces. The coke, oxygen and firing processes were all too unpredictable to guarantee quality beyond a certain level. Within a short period of time this was changed, as the random variations began to come more under control and the standards were progressively tightened. More significantly the improvement in performance within the central melting plant began to result in a reduction in production costs and improvements in the quality of the finished pipes. Put another way, the internal costs of failure, the external costs of failure and the costs of appraisal began to decrease. The change in attitudes is also a good example of how, in Juran's model, an organization can move from control to breakthrough.

One of the keys to success was the use of some simple statistical techniques which will be covered later under training (see Chapter 12). What is more critical is the importance of understanding that statistics play an important although often overrated role in total quality. It does explain to a large extent some of the reasons behind the Japanese dominance because of their concentration on the use of simple statistical techniques. Certainly the statistical control of variation is one of the key factors in Japan's success in setting quality standards and underlay most of the movement which was introduced by Deming.

Much more important, the long-term reward of diagnosing quality costs in the way described is the complete elimination of the inspection function other than that carried out during normal line operations. This of course is a long-term process, as has been mentioned before. Canon Cameras in Japan achieved over a 15-year programme of total quality management the complete elimination of the inspection function. This provided a stark contrast to one of the earliest total quality assignments in which I was involved. The client was a major defence contractor but also a household name in a range of products. During the early 1980s the plant concerned had a good reputation for quality, but the cost of that quality was enormous. In one of the key machine rooms, where the product had to be produced to the highest specifications, quality standards were achieved by endless reworking and by tight inspection rules on everything that was produced. It was only with the introduction of a total quality programme linked to a proper diagnosis of quality costs that management began to realize the scale of the quality cost and why they were having significant competitive problems in the market place. Today the plant is one of the most profitable parts of the organization in question, to a large extent because of the significant drive to reduce quality costs while maintaining the highest quality standards.

I have considered the approach to quality costs in some depth because as part of the strategic development of any total quality programme it is essential for the organization to have a real understanding of quality costs. Without this understanding it is difficult to persuade both senior management and indeed all other parts of the organization that there are some real challenges to be faced and, as has been demonstrated in a number of examples, a real need for change of attitude. A detailed analysis of quality costs can shock organizations into action. In particular by a detailed analysis in the diagnostic phase it is possible:

- to identify the real costs of quality
- to understand in broad terms what can be directly eliminated (assignable causes) and what needs to be controlled (random variations)
- to recognize the importance of at least some basic statistical techniques.

People and attitudes

Any programme of change is likely to bring resistance, however progressive and forward looking an organization may be. Consider the possible implications of a total quality programme:

- reductions in numbers, such as inspectors or those involved in complaints administration
- changes of management style with greater devolvement of responsibility – this may often be seen as a threat, particularly by middle management, with typical worries such as:
  - a long list of problems is being identified when middle managers have spent a great deal of effort convincing top management that they have no problems
  - a problem is solved relatively easily with large cost savings when middle management have not been able to solve it and/or have not been aware of the problem
- a lack of knowledge of the techniques used within total quality, particularly the concern about learning new statistical techniques
- a more participative approach whereby middle management have less control over some of the activities involved in total quality such as task groups or quality circles.

As this shows and as Juran, Deming and others have indicated, a total quality programme demands a radical shift in management attitudes. The changes in attitude required are of course not confined to management but are also required of the work force generally at all levels.

While recognizing this need for change, the top management of an organization may well not have full detailed understanding of current attitudes and the prevailing culture within their own organization. In my experience there is much mythology among top management about the organization climate. It is important therefore that as part of the strategic development there is a diagnosis of the prevailing organization climate. The importance of this has been recognized in so many different examples, particularly those used by Peters and Waterman in their study *In Search of Excellence* where considerable emphasis is placed on creating the appropriate organization culture and positive attitudes to quality. Of the many examples quoted in *In Search of Excellence* one that was particularly striking involved the MacDonalds organization. Despite the franchise nature of the operation and the large distribution of individual sites it was possible to create a commitment to quality standards by creating the right climate within the organization. This was also recognized by Peter Wickens in *The Road to Nissan,*[3] but of course Nissan had the opportunity to build their own organization culture on a greenfield site – difficult for most existing organizations. The Japanese have also recognized this and spent a great deal of time developing the positive attitudes to total quality within an organization.

The most effective way of understanding prevailing attitudes within an organization is to carry out an organization climate survey. In particular it is important to determine whether there are differences in attitudes between different parts and levels of the organization.

Using results from a questionnaire, Figure 8 sets out a comparison within a major seafood organization comparing the site director's view of the climate where the initial total quality programme was developed (prior to its introduction), with the view of the senior site management. The results show that:

● the site director considered he had a devolved management style which allowed initiative within reasonably clear goals
● the site director recognized that there were particular problems in team identification and work standards

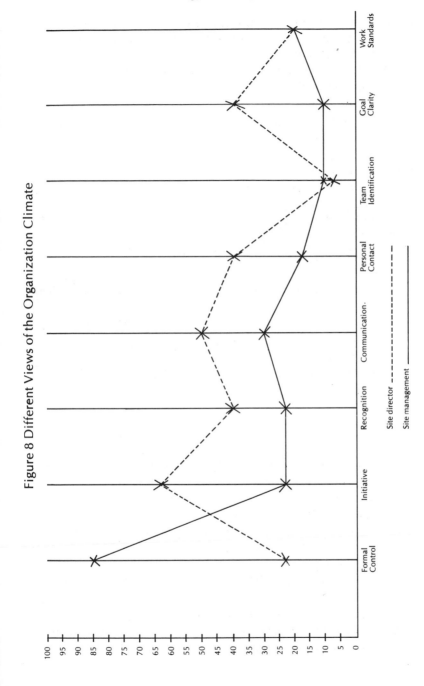

Figure 8 Different Views of the Organization Climate

- the site management had significantly contrasting views on management style and initiative but also felt communication and lack of clear objectives were major problems
- there was agreement with the site director that attitudes to work standards were not positive.

This type of analysis – showing in particular the differences in perception – enables a total quality programme to be developed taking account of the prevailing attitudes. In this case, for instance, it was clear that particular emphasis would have to be put on ensuring the style of management from the top allowed site management to take more initiative in managing the total quality programme. This was done by ensuring they were responsible for developing the actual implementation programme as a team, which also had the effect of improving teamwork and clarifying objectives.

The advantages of using this approach or indeed other similar approaches at the strategic development phase are:

- it provides data on attitudes prevailing within an organization
- it forces top management and subsequently other levels to accept that attitudes may not be as positive and open to change as might have been thought. I was much struck on one occasion by a speaker at a conference which was about communications within organizations. The speaker was talking about the so-called chairman's annual message within internal newspapers or magazines. He indicated that the last person who should actually write the chairman's message was the chairman who in many organizations insisted that he understood how management and the work force really ticked. The reality is that in many cases this is completely wrong and there are some considerable gaps between the views on the organization of the chairman and of the rest. This particularly applies to attitudes about quality
- it helps the design of a total quality programme which is not only able to reflect company needs, having identified particular problem areas in terms of both attitudes and potential difficulties in implementation, but also avoids the packaged approach to total quality implementation.

Developing a strategy without understanding the prevailing attitudes within an organization is likely to lead to major problems in its implementation and possibly ultimate failure. Many consultants have fallen into the trap of developing glossy packages for the implementation of total quality which they hawk to different organizations working in different sectors. While many of the principles will apply, as has already been indicated, it is essential that any approach to total quality is tailored to meet the needs of a particular organization. These needs can be identified more clearly by carrying out organization climate surveys and providing a framework for action. To develop strategies without a full understanding of the facts about an organization in terms of people and attitudes is similar to implementing a total quality programme without understanding the costs of quality. No management would consider a total quality programme without a detailed analysis of quality costs. The same applies to the need for a detailed analysis of attitudes.

I would also emphasize that the benefits of carrying out surveys of this kind can only be effective in the long run if they are followed up on a regular basis with similar surveys. The success of a total quality programme cannot only be measured by the obvious business benefits of the changes as a result of improved quality performance. The long-term benefits, as for instance an organization moves from the stage of uncertainty through enlightenment to certainty can to a large extent be measured not only by the specific actions outlined by Crosby but by changes in attitudes. An example of such changes can be seen in Figure 9 which shows how the site director and the site managment in the seafoods organization moved from some significant differences of view about the prevailing climate on the site towards greater consensus over a period of twelve months as the total quality programme began to take effect. Additionally there were significant and positive changes particularly in attitudes to work standards.

The organization climate survey provides a good foundation in helping to understand attitudes and possible resistances to change. Equally important is to review effectiveness by carrying out an organizational effectiveness audit. The issues which require addressing in such an audit would include:

(a) a review of the work environment which would take account of:

● organization structure – looking at the hierarchy within the organization, the extent to which responsibilities are divided

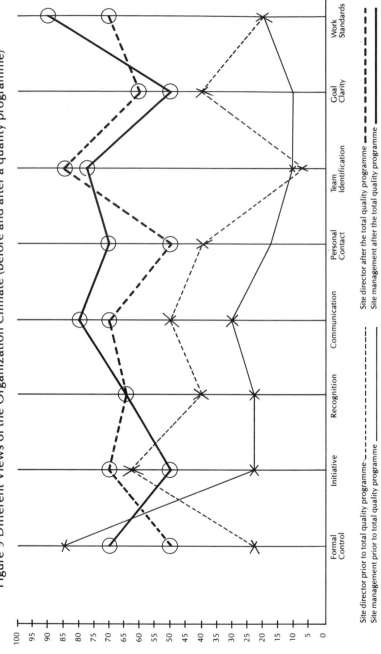

Figure 9 Different Views of the Organization Climate (before and after a quality programme)

Site director prior to total quality programme - - - - - - -   Site director after the total quality programme - - - - -
Site management prior to total quality programme _____   Site management after the total quality programme _____

up, the separation between direct and indirect departments, possible overlaps and duplication
- work organization – looking within departments, particularly at how work is divided and organized
- decision making processes and the extent to which decision making is delegated or the high level bureaucratic processes whereby decision making is centralized in a few key areas
- communications – the effectiveness of communications both within and between departments and whether the existing vehicles really work, the extent to which top management actually promotes good communications, whether employees feel well informed
- physical conditions – the general environment in which people work
- pay structure – is it likely to promote or inhibit commitment to quality standards or is there an incentive oriented style where production rather than quality is important?
- trade union relations – looking at the present state of industrial relations within the organization and the extent to which the trade unions are likely to co-operate with a total quality programme.

(b) technology and techniques which apply within the organization and which may affect the implementation of a total quality programme including:

- cost control – methods and systems for controlling costs within the organization
- production planning – the extent to which there is an effective production planning process within the organization
- marketing – particularly the structure of the marketing department and how it relates to the external and internal contacts essential to successful marketing
- technology – the extent to which technology has been introduced and possible future plans.

(c) the individual – looking in particular at how individuals within the organization are considered with particular reference to:

- recruitment and selection techniques and the extent to which positive efforts are made to try to generate proper fits between new employees and the skills required

● training and management development with particular reference to skills training, growth of knowledge and emphasis on development of positive attitudes.

The approach outlined in Figure 10, when combined with the organization climate, provides a framework for linking people and quality within an organization by determining existing levels of job satisfaction and effectiveness, the industrial relations climate and quality programme and all its constituent parts.

Customer requirements

The third major strand of the strategy development phase of any total quality programme is to examine in depth customer requirements. With the fundamental concept of quality based on meeting customer requirements, it is essential to be clear on those requirements. As I have already indicated in a number of examples, the definition of customer requirements can be difficult. Lack of emphasis on this particular stage can undermine a total quality programme, however well organized. There are a number of different elements in considering requirements and these are set out below.

Identify customers/clients

At the strategic level and taking account of the external relationships for an organization it is necessary to define:

● The market – for instance, in the electrical goods industry does the organization operate at the expensive end (such as Sony could be defined as operating) or at the cheaper end of the market (such as Saisho). In both cases there are quality standards to be met and cheapness should not be interpreted as shoddiness or poor quality.
● Who is the customer/client in a particular situation? For instance, in the food industry, particularly in packaged foods, there are potentially two customers, the supermarket and the individual customer of the supermarket. Within a major seafoods organization these two customers were clearly defined.

Figure 10 Linking People and Quality

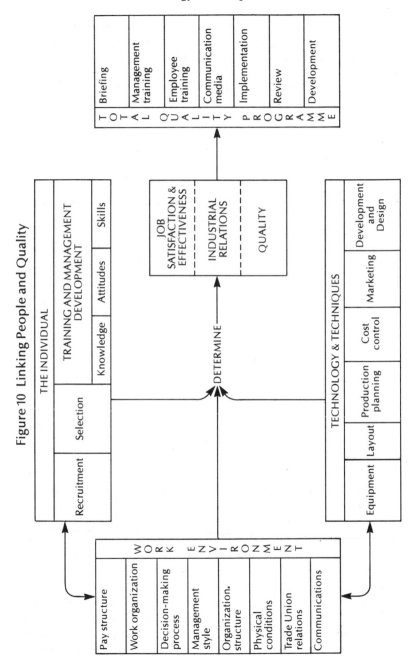

The supermarket customer required quality standards which in particular emphasized delivery reliability, lack of damage to packaging and to some extent attractive packaging. The individual customer buying the product on the supermarket shelf tended to emphasize quality of product. Both these customers had to be serviced and quality standards defined to take account of both these sets of needs.

● Customer quality priorities are also important to determine because quite often individual organizations will impose their own priorities on customer requirements. One way of determining priorities is to carry out a customer survey as was done in the major programme to improve the performance of SAS, the Scandanavian airline. The whole company strategy for revival and quality standards was based on what were identified as the key needs for the business passenger. In manufacturing industry there are many ways of monitoring customer and quality priorities. Mullard, which is part of the Philips group, identified the importance of having some simple measure of quality performance. The company concluded that the worst possible situation was that a complaint about any aspect of their performance was sufficiently serious to warrant a customer writing, telexing or even having to telephone the company with a problem. As a result Mullard adopted a measure called 'adverse quality communication' (AQC) which included all methods of communication to the organization about something which was wrong. As a result, as part of their strategy development, a target could be set based on percentage improvement per annum against a base. The results could then be carefully monitored. This was a useful management tool for monitoring customer performance in an organization with a mixture of product types.

Within an organization's so-called quality network we have already identified the customer/supplier relationship. In determining the strategy for total quality it is also essential to have a mechanism for monitoring quality standards and quality improvements within the organization. One method of doing this is to ask all departmental managers to review functional responsibilities and ensure that the departmental objectives match the business objectives. This is achieved by first carrying out a detailed analytical review of departmental activities with the emphasis being placed on specific objectives and targets, and secondly by structured and objective analysis of the service given by the particular department to an 'internal' customer. The specific results from such a survey include:

- a statement of departmental purpose in terms of specific objectives
- an opportunity to ensure that these objectives match the company and organizational objectives
- a quantitative analysis of departmental activity measured under the main objective headings and major tasks – this is possible both within service departments and within direct production departments
- an objective assessment of departmental effectiveness as seen by an internal customer
- a set of key performance measures – the outcome of determining the key departmental activities and the internal customer requirements
- the basis for an improvement plan
- a list of non-added value or wasted work performed by the department.

The actual methodology used to go through this process can vary according to individual organizations and the degree of sophistication required at any point. A simple way forward is for the departmental manager to meet with all the individuals directly reporting to him or her, probably for an uninterrupted whole day in the first place. At this meeting the following process can be adopted:

(a) the departmental manager outlines his or her individual roles and responsibilities and what he or she sees to be the main objectives of the department;

(b) the group as a whole then discuss the roles and responsibilities clarifying issues and as appropriate making changes of emphasis and achieving consensus;

(c) each individual in the group is then required to go through the same process outlining their roles and responsibilities with discussions following – this enables the team as a whole to clarify areas of overlap and to establish a clear idea of the responsibilities both individually and as a group;

(d) at the end of this process it is possible to:
- identify the objectives of the department
- check whether the department objectives meet the overall company/organizational objectives
- provide a framework for analysis by an internal customer against customer requirements.

(e) after this stage the departmental manager then outlines in specific quantitative terms the 'outputs' that he or she will be required to deliver as an individual as well as the 'outputs' of the department as a whole – in other words the quantitative analysis of what is required of the department and the measures for ensuring such objectives can be monitored at the end of an appropriate period;

(f) each individual also carries out the same process explaining their 'outputs' to the team as a whole;

(g) at the end of the process the department has moved from broad definitions of responsibilities to specific measurable outputs which need to be achieved;

(h) the documentation arising from this process is then pulled together and produced for discussion with internal customers and for review by top management.

Liaison with customers

Identifying the market and customer requirements is the first stage of a review of customers within the organization. Once this has been done a close and regular liaison should be established with customers to monitor any changes and to ensure there is an understanding at the technical level of the requirements. An example of this often quoted is Jaguar Cars who regularly ring up customers to establish whether there are any individual difficulties or problems with the product and to determine whether there is any particular need for action or change. More recently Ford have established a similar system based particularly on the company car drivers who form an increasingly large part of the new car market. This includes regular surveys of customer requirements. In addition to this, there is a need to establish technical standards which reflect customer needs. BS 5750 provides an excellent framework for doing this and for establishing with customers that the organization has a basic framework of quality standards. Another example of the need to have this technical liaison is well demonstrated in Japan with the customer/supplier relationship in the motor industry. The ability of the suppliers of components to meet customer requirements defined by specific quality standards can only be achieved by regular visits to the assembly lines to identify and deal with particular problems and difficulties.

In establishing a close liaison with customers a number of key factors need to be agreed as follows:

(a) what the customer expects in terms of 'deliverables': the detailed specifications in terms of price, quality, delivery dates and so on so that there can be no misunderstanding;

(b) the actual quality standards that are required by the customer and how these will be measured – for instance, tolerance levels on components, what is acceptable and not acceptable, packaging for consumer goods, the flexibility if any in delivery times and dates;

(c) methods that will be used to measure the quality standards – this particularly applies to the quality network within an organization but is also important with external customers – the use of statistical techniques and other methods provide a foundation for establishing how measurement will be carried out. For instance, at Canon Cameras in Japan it was apparent that there was only sample inspection of the finished cameras. Although it was not possible to identify the level of sampling it was clear from conversations with the Japanese management that there was agreement with the customers (the wholesalers) of the amount of sample testing that was taking place. The extent to which this varied depended on the overall quality standards of the product;

(d) it is also important to establish the current level of performance in specific terms so that there is a clear base from which to build – the AQC system in Mullard provided a good base to enable organizations to measure improvements in performance;

(e) finally a clear understanding of reporting methods on quality standards and level of performance with the customer is essential to ensure there exists a clear method for reviewing performance – again BS 5750 provides a useful framework for this.

Strategy development – conclusions

The strategy development phase of an implementation programme is based on establishing and understanding the quality issues within the organization. Primarily it is aimed at ensuring that top management have a clear view of the quality costs, the attitudes of management and the work force and customer requirements. This gives a basis for strategy development by providing a focus for change and determining clearly what the mission and objectives of a total quality programme will be. Establishing this as a clear statement from top management is an essential prerequisite of any total quality programme. It provides a statement of the values that will apply within the organization and also provides an indication of top management commitment to the total quality programme. Figure 11 sets out the processes involved.

Figure 11 Strategy Development

Perhaps more important is that by defining clearly the new strategy based on the implementation of total quality, top management are able to articulate the direction of the organization. This can then be compared at least in general terms with the existing performance levels and attitudes applying within the organization. The difference between the new strategy and the existing situation I define as the development gap (see Figure 12). The successful implementation programme centres on tackling the development gap by recognizing the individual needs of an organization. This provides a framework for the strategy which can be clearly understood by top management and can be measured in terms of determining whether changes and improvements have taken place.

Figure 12 The Development Gap

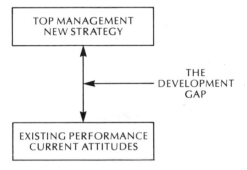

Once the strategy development stage has been carried out a firm foundation has been set for the next stage – planning for action. Experience has shown that the strategy development phase can take up to two years. Using the Crosby model, this period takes an organization from the uncertainty stage, where there is no realization that there is even a problem, to the awakening stage where a strategy begins to emerge. Top management must lead this stage because their commitment can only be achieved by a full understanding of the issues involved. Within Rank Xerox, for instance, the period from the beginning of major difficulties in the market place to the point at which top management launched the total quality programme was several years. From about 1980 cost reductions were implemented and while this was happening Xerox top management were beginning to make other fundamental changes. In particular more attention was placed on the products, services and practices of the competition which established key criteria for performance. During 1981 and 1982 the strategy development was beginning to take shape and, having set the targets, the problem was to ensure that all levels within the organization responded to the targets. Finally, in February 1983 the top management of Xerox began to pull the strategy together by establishing the focus for change – leadership through quality – and established the mission statement which ran as follows: 'Xerox is a quality company. Quality is a basic business principle for Xerox. Quality means providing our external and internal customers with innovative products and services to fully satisfy their requirements. Quality improvement is the job of every Xerox employee.'

From this statement it was possible to identify the development gap and from there to prepare a strategy which resulted in a major training programme, which was to run through until late 1987. The Xerox story provides a good illustration of how the implementation of total quality is a long-term process, as so strongly advocated and practised by the Japanese.

Chapter 10
PLANNING FOR ACTION

We have now laid the foundation through the strategy development phase for beginning the preparation for the implementation of total quality. In particular we have identified the 'development gap' which provides a framework for the planning stage of S-P-O based on an identification of quality costs, the culture and attitudes within the organization and the customer requirements.

Having carried out this diagnosis top management are inevitably anxious to begin implementation. While this anxiety is understandable because of the business pressures, the planning stage is probably the most critical part of the implementation programme. The pressures to deliver often mean that insufficient attention is paid to this phase, as a result of which many total quality programmes have encountered difficulties during the implementation stage or have even begun to fall apart. This pressure is often illustrated at the time top management decide to use external consultants to help them with the implementation programme. In my direct experience I have found that when being asked to assist management with implementation the assumption is that since they have decided – ie. the strategy development phase – to implement a total quality programme, all that is needed is external help to facilitate, as an additional resource and expertise, the implementation stage. I have often encountered frustration and at times hostility when I have suggested that it is essential in any total quality programme to go through the detailed planning phase. The main reason for this is that, having carried out a detailed diagnosis of the situation, any programme must be tailored to meet the needs of a particular organization, both in operational and in cultural terms. There has been a tendency among external consultants to produce a packaged total quality programme which often looks glossy and contains a great deal of detailed training material. While many of the elements are probably suitable for cross-training between different organizations and different sectors in the economy, positive adjustments and tailoring are needed to ensure effective implementation. The planning phase helps to eliminate the packaged approach and to ensure, as far as is practicable, that an effective programme is developed.

There are three parts to the planning for action phase, as follows:

● management of the programme
● design of training programmes
● implementation timetable.

These are considered in more detail below.

Management of the programme

Any management of change programme not only requires the broad commitment of top management but also needs some specific responsibilities to be established at key levels within the organization. These can be achieved in the following way and require action during the planning phase so that the overall planning of the programme can be developed. The key is to establish clear levels of responsibility, as follows:

(a) at board level or at the highest strategic level within the organization an individual director or equivalent must be given specific responsibility for the total quality programme. This responsibility requires high publicity and demonstrates commitment at the highest level. Specific responsibilities at this level include:

● overseeing the planning phase of the programme
● establishing criteria for measuring success
● monitoring performance against criteria
● providing overall leadership of the programme, in particular by maintaining high visibility and ensuring that top management colleagues are continuously reminded of the need to support the programme – this role could be replicated in very large organizations at a divisional management level but only if it is a director level appointment;

(b) the appointment of a senior manager with specific responsibility for the total quality programme – unlike the board level appointment which is part of wider responsibilities, this is a full time role with complete responsibility for the total quality programme. It should be emphasized that the responsibility is a supportive role and unlike the traditional role of the quality manager who was often seen as being responsible for quality. The total quality manager is responsible for overseeing the implementation of the programme. It may be recalled that in Japan it is unusual even to have a quality department because quality is seen clearly as the responsibility of line management. The prime responsibility of the quality manager is to support the programme, train all levels and monitor quality performance by:

- providing advice and guidance to line management on all aspects of the total quality programme
- contributing to strategic planning particularly in relation to total quality
- managing the training process at all levels and (depending on the size of the organization) carrying out much of the training
- providing data on quality performance.

The appointment of the total quality manager is critical to the success of the whole programme because it requires a senior manager who has both a great deal of experience and commands much respect within the organization. Equally it should be emphasized again that this is not a replacement of the old fashioned chief inspector by another name. The individual should report direct to the board of the organization;

(c) the establishment of a steering committee or what Crosby calls a quality improvement team: the responsibilities of this team are to provide a forum for overseeing the day to day management of the total quality programme and to bring together the main departments within the organization. The responsibilities of this team would include:

- detailed review of the objectives of the programme and the concepts involved
- management of the total quality programme
- monitoring of the overall progress of the programme.

The quality improvement team provides a forum for debate,

discussion and action. It should be emphasized strongly, however, that the team does not have direct responsibility for implementation of the programme within individual departments and acts primarily as a forum for the total quality manager to consult. It also provides a high level and high profile forum for the programme.

While these three levels of responsibility are necessary, the specific details need to be determined to meet the requirements of a particular organization and thus two issues immediately arise. The above approach reflects a typical organization within the private sector and there is often debate whether it is possible to extend this approach into the public sector. Public sector organizations who essentially act like private companies usually have a structure within which the above responsibilities can be established. Examples of such organizations might include the CEGB or British Rail. However within, for instance, local government this becomes more difficult because it is difficult to establish clearly levels of responsibility and decision making. The French experience would indicate that at local government level it is possible to identify an *elected* officer of government who will take responsibility for the programme which is the equivalent of the board level responsibility. While the way this responsibility may be handled is different, the concept remains the same. The appointment of a senior council officer with special responsibilities for total quality can easily be established and reflect normal divisional responsibilities within local authorities. The steering group is usually made up of local officers rather than elected officials and represents those who have day to day responsibility within the council rather than elected responsibility. Similar patterns have been found in other public sector applications such as the health service within the UK.

The second aspect which needs some debate is the establishment of a steering group or quality improvement team. While it is difficult to generalize, I have found that the establishment of such a team does not always help a total quality programme because it creates an environment where the programme is seen as something different from the normal management processes and could be counterproductive. Usually the need for such a group is much clearer in very large organizations where it is necessary to provide a focus and a forum for the total quality programme. It is a means of establishing common standards, practices and ensuring that the quality of the training programme is consistent across the whole organization. Within smaller organizations the management team itself is capable of providing such a focus. The danger of this is that the details of the programme may get lost when considered with all the other operating issues which tend to be raised at senior management level. The greatest advantage is that it integrates the total quality programme into the normal management processes.

It is not really possible to prescribe the most appropriate approach. All the major influences on the quality movement advocate that there should be some central focus. Many of the outstanding examples of success also indicate that such an approach is useful, particularly in the early part of a programme. However, as already mentioned, the Japanese tend not to have a steering group because total quality is seen so clearly as part of line management. Also it is worth noting that Peters and Waterman in their book *In Search of Excellence* indicate that the most effective groups of this kind are those which exist only for a limited time.

The conclusion probably is that in general the establishment of a steering group or quality improvement team is an important factor in the setting up of a total quality programme and the early monitoring of that programme. Once the programme is well established within the organization (perhaps some four or five years after the commencement of the programme) it should be possible, and is probably good practice, to merge the team into the normal management processes. By that time the total quality programme should have a momentum of its own, although the merging process needs to be handled carefully to ensure that it is not misinterpreted as the end of the programme.

Design of different training programmes

The detailed diagnosis carried out during the strategy development phase provides a good foundation for the development of training programmes. In essence the diagnosis could be described as a detailed training needs analysis for all levels within the organization which can then be matched against the needs of the total quality programme. Once again the concept of the development gap is the key to the success of the training programmes.

The design of the training programme must therefore be based on an understanding of the development gap, which may be very different, as these two examples show:

The mass male toiletries organization already referred to was undergoing rapid growth, had a management style which was based on short-term firefighting (Juran's control), was marketing led and, despite its many successes, was badly organized with poor discipline. For instance, I remember sitting through one key management team meeting lasting five hours, where three hours were spent arguing about the facts. On the other hand the organization was dynamic, a market leader and responded well to change.

The second was a major telecommunications organization which was characterized by bureaucracy and considerable resistance to change, and whose training was largely systems driven rather than customer oriented.

The design of the training programmes for these two organizations needed to reflect their particular needs and no standard package could in itself meet these needs without considerable tailoring.

In essence, training in a total quality programme is a combination of three factors:

● management skills training
● techniques training (particularly statistical techniques)
● corporate culture development.

It can be seen that it is both necessary and possible to tailor the training to meet individual organizational needs. The planning phase provides the opportunity to tailor individual programmes to meet organizational needs and it is essential for the long-term success of the total quality programme. As already indicated, except possibly for very small organizations where it may be expensive to carry out detailed tailoring of programmes, a packaged approach tends to be counterproductive. There are probably four levels of training within a typical programme, covering:

● top management
● management
● task group leaders
● facilitators.

The objectives for each will vary to meet the particular needs of that level as follows:

For top management the objectives of a typical workshop would be to:

- provide an introduction to total quality management within an organization
- provide an appreciation of the main processes and techniques used in total quality management
- agree an action programme for the organization including key objectives, responsibilities and outline programme.

For management the workshop objectives would be similar to the first two objectives for top management (but provided in a lot more detail) and thirdly:

- to design a detailed implementation programme for individual areas of the organization.

The difference between the management workshop and the top management workshop is that the management workshop would have specific responsibility for designing the implementation programme in detail, as opposed to the overall strategy, which would be the responsibility of top management. Involvement of both of these groups is critical to the success of the programme because it provides ownership at critical operational levels and ensures the programme reflects operating reality. In Juran's terms it moves management from control to breakthrough.

For task group leaders the training objectives for members of the steering group/quality improvement team as well as for individual task group leaders at departmental level or even in problem-solving groups include:

- to ensure that group leaders understand the total quality programme and how it will work within the organization
- to assist leaders to appreciate and use a range of leadership and interpersonal skills appropriate to effective group working
- to assist leaders to understand some of the analytical methods and statistical techniques used in total quality
- to help leaders improve their communication skills and gain confidence in making presentations
- to ensure that task group leaders are aware of the resources available within the company to help them.

This course is probably the core course of the whole programme.

For facilitators (including the total quality manager) who would be responsible for providing support and guidance to the total quality programme and in particular problem-solving groups within the programme, it may be necessary to run a specialized workshop with the following objectives:

- to understand the role of the facilitator
- to increase knowledge of behavioural and communication styles
- to agree on the practical arrangements.

The planning phase not only includes the design of the above programmes but also requires detailed identification of:

- the individuals and groups likely to attend each level – this may seem a simple process but the success of the programmes can often be affected by ensuring that the appropriate levels attend each programme in order to gain maximum benefit and create the greatest synergy
- those responsible for providing the training – typically one would expect either an extremely senior member of management or, more likely, external consultants to provide the training at the highest level and probably train the internal trainers to deliver the detailed programmes at the lower levels – either way the resourcing of training is critical
- those responsible for the actual detailed development of the training programmes, including the appropriate case studies, which to be successful must be tailored to the needs of the particular organization.

The details of the training programme outlined above are considered in Chapter 12.

Development of Detailed Timetable

The implementation of a total quality programme involving the whole organization requires meticulous planning and detailed timetabling. This phase is the final stage of the planning process when a great deal of the detailed preparation has already been carried out as indicated previously. In devising a detailed timetable there are probably some critical activities which influence the whole timetable and which can form the basis of that programme. It is difficult to generalize because the timetable is affected by the size of the organization and the amount of detailed briefing that needs to be provided within an organization. These key activities include:

- the public launch date of the programme
- the key training dates
- the implementation dates for task groups
- the initial review dates.

The purpose of developing a detailed programme which can be announced as part of the launch is primarily to show commitment as well as to pin people down and generate their commitment. Experience has also shown that there is a certain cycle to the implementation of a programme. For instance I found that launch dates much after early June or late November tend to be ineffective and the momentum of programmes can be lost because of the summer and Christmas holiday periods. Additionally, the cycle of work in an organization can influence the timing of a particular programme. So what are the key elements of a detailed timetable? An example of a launch programme may provide an indication and a framework for developing individual timetables.

The company in question was the mass male toiletries organization. The launch of the total quality programme was based, being essentially a marketing organization, on the concept of the product launch. The company decided that the total quality programme, which was to be called 'Pride', would be launched on 12 May. My detailed discussion with the company began in early February. The requirements included:

- establishing a pre-launch timetable
- designing the outline programme
- agreeing the programme with top management
- running two management workshops to brief senior middle management and with them design a detailed implementation programme
- set up the post-launch implementation programme.

All this had to be agreed before early March. The pre-launch action required the running of the two management workshops for the individual site management in a way that prevented too many rumours among management on the two sites and did not pre-empt the effect of the launch on 12 May. Thus the workshops were run in the week before 12 May, which left very little time to prepare a detailed post-launch programme.

After the launch on 12 May it was necessary to carry out detailed briefing at site level in the week commencing 19 May as a prelude to running the task group leader training courses in the early part of June. After the completion of the training the total quality programme was launched for real with the initial review due to be carried out on 1 October.

These stages demonstrate that in an organization which had:

Figure 13 A Typical Implementation Programme

	DECISION TO IMPLEMENT
MONTH 1	Detailed Briefing of Senior Management Review of organizational needs established through strategy phase
MONTH 2	Outline design of implementation
MONTH 3	Management workshops to design detailed implementation programme
MONTH 4	Launch of Programme – Publicity – Detailed Briefing
MONTH 5	Establishment of Task Groups. Pilot Improvement Groups
MONTH 6	Completion of initial pilot projects

- already decided to implement a total quality programme, having completed the strategic phase
- decided upon the formal launch date within the organization
- achieved broad top management support to the concept of introducing a total quality programme,

an elapsed time of six months was necessary from the point at which the decision was made to implement total quality to completion of the first stage. This was within an organization which was comparatively small, with two sites employing 450 people. Larger ones, particularly those operating on a multi-national basis, would require significantly longer periods of time just for the implementation programme.

Figure 13 sets out a typical implementation programme.

The second phase of a total quality programme has involved 'planning for action', which incorporates:

- establishing the management processes for the programme
- providing a framework for the training programme
- preparing a detailed timetable.

At this point an organization is able to move to the third phase of S-P-O, the operating elements.

Chapter 11
OPERATING ELEMENTS – BRIEFING

We have completed the first two phases of the total quality implementation programme: strategy development and planning. We can now move to the operating elements, the third phase of the S-P-O approach to quality. As an organization moves to this phase it already has in place:

- an overall strategy/mission
- a plan for implementation which includes
  - specific responsibilities for the programme
  - training and briefing programme design
  - an overall timetable.

The framework is now in place to press the button for implementation. In broad terms there are four major stages in an implementation programme:

- briefing
- training
- implementation
- review.

These are considered in detail below.

Briefing

The purpose of the briefing phase is to launch the total quality programme across an organization. A great deal of preparatory work has already taken place and this launch enables top management to demonstrate publicly its commitment to the programme and to outline the main elements of it. It also provides the basis for launching the specific elements of the programme by providing some general information on how it will operate.

The actual design of the launch programme needs to take account of existing systems within the organization for communication, the culture and of course the size of the organization. There will probably be two stages of this briefing programme, the initial launch briefing and the detailed briefing at departmental or equivalent level.

At one extreme is the 'big bang' approach to the initial briefing. An outstanding example of this was the mass male toiletries organization which as already indicated launched their total quality awareness programme, called 'Pride', like a product launch, familiar to an organization which had successfully launched a range of products in the previous five years. The company had three broad groups of people involved, the head office staff which included all the brand managers and support staff based in Berkshire, the factory staff and product support staff based in the North East and the sales force which covered the majority of the country. The company invited all employees from all sites for the major launch which was to be held in Newcastle Civic Centre. This was the first time that all employees had been brought together in a single place. The launch of the programme had been prepared by the marketing department in consultation with the company's advertising agency.

The launch was introduced by the managing director, who then handed over to the two presenters from the BBC television programme *Tomorrow's World*. This had the advantage of not only providing a thoroughly professional presentation but also creating an immediate impact with everybody present. The launch programme was based on the PRIDE concept representing:

Pace – indicating a fast-moving consumer goods company
Responsibility – emphasizing that everybody has responsibility to contribute
Initiative – encouraging everybody to contribute to the company's objectives
Development – showing how everybody will be involved and gain personally in the long term
Everybody – emphasizing that every single member of the company had a contribution to make.

Interviews were shown on video involving all levels of the organization from the shop floor to the managing director. All the interviews indicated long-term commitment to the organization and an emphasis that the organization was changing and growing and developing. During the course of these interviews it was possible also to show some of the new investment in the company facilities, particularly a new automated warehouse which was due to be opened as part of the launch programme and a visible manifestation of the company's longer-term commitment. The final element of the presentation brought in a number of the basic elements which were to form part of the total quality programme. In particular:

- the launch of a new company newspaper, which was called PRIDE and in its first edition, distributed during the presentation, inevitably featured the total quality programme
- the introduction of 'pace and intensity' awards, rewards of high visibility but relatively little cost, to be given to individuals who had made an outstanding contribution to the total quality programme
- the setting up of a senior project team, called Project Ascent, which consisted primarily of the top management of the organization and effectively was the steering committee for the total quality programme
- the launch of 'Improvement Groups' which were the problem-solving groups set up at local level as part of the total quality programme.

The presentation, which lasted some 40 minutes in total, created a framework of ideas, concepts and actions which were going to form part of the programme in the future. This was aimed in particular at dealing with the likely cynicism which might arise from such a spectacular launch programme in the long run. There were indications of future action which when they were actually carried out later helped to convince the cynics that the company really was going to change and implement a series of initiatives as part of the programme.

The reaction of the employees was generally positive. Of course there was much cynicism both about the expenditure and about whether anything would actually happen. In some ways the impact of the presentation grew greater as time went past and a programme was implemented. The employees began to see changes in the organization as they themselves became more involved in many aspects of the programme.

A number of useful lessons can be drawn from this particular approach, as follows:

● a spectacular approach of this kind not only needs a great deal of planning and involves a high level of expenditure but also needs to be followed quickly by action, otherwise in the long run it will be completely counter-productive
● the approach itself reflected the prevailing culture in the organization which was very market driven – employees were used to the high quality advertisements for the company's products
● the size of the organization permitted a spectacular launch – there are very few organizations which are either small enough or are able/willing effectively to take a whole day out of production and selling activity in order to launch such a programme.

No less planning is necessary for launches of total quality programmes which perhaps require a lower key approach.

Many organizations will launch their total quality programme by a series of cascade briefings, beginning with top management's agreement on the way to move forward. They in turn brief the senior managers and over a period of time the total quality programme is launched. This low-key approach, favoured by many, has the advantage of often avoiding some of the cynicism of the higher impact approaches, as outlined in the example above. Nevertheless there is a need for a focus to the launch of the programme and this can be done using the appropriate media which currently exist in the organization. The majority for instance, will have some form of company newspaper, however much it may be regarded as a sinecure or 'emasculated of any real views'. It can provide a focus for the launch of the programme by the production of a special edition which explains:

● the mission/objective of the programme
● the reasons why senior management have launched the programme
● the details of the key elements of the programme – steering committee, responsibility for different aspects of the programme, the broad timetable
● in general terms how employees may be involved in the programme.

If there is no company newsletter/newspaper then the opportunity can be taken either to launch one as part of an on-going communication programme linked to total quality, or to have a 'one-off' publication which launches the programme. The published document needs to be easy to read and should not create an atmosphere of concern, for instance among the middle managers who may be undermined, or among all levels because there is some fear of redundancy. Technical details of the programme should also be avoided at this stage. The presentation needs to be positive, emphasizing that the total quality programme is something which is in everybody's interest and provides a foundation for the future development and growth of the organization. If appropriate, it can also make reference to other similar organizations which have adopted a total quality programme showing the benefits that have been achieved.

As part of the major launch top management in those organizations which are unionized must recognize the importance of involving the trade unions in the programme launch. A special briefing of the trade union representatives ahead of the major launch is important in order to ensure that they do not undermine the programme. One of my early experiences of a total quality programme involved a major defence contractor which was highly unionized. Management made the mistake of creating the environment whereby the discussions on the total quality programme effectively became negotiable. The unions quickly insisted that unless management were prepared to concede to some other demands (which were totally unrelated but which had been under discussion for some time) then they would not cooperate with the total quality programme. Total quality is about the management of an organization and is the responsibility of management to implement. I have found that using the normal channels of communication with the trade unions wherever practicable is the most effective way of involving them in the process.

Additionally, consideration can be given, depending on the structure of the steering committee, to trade union representation on the steering committee, although if the steering committee is effectively the top management team it is unlikely to be appropriate that there should be trade union representation at this level. Of course they are also likely to be involved as individuals in task groups and problem solving groups at departmental level. In the example (described elsewhere) of chemical works, a trade union representative led a quality circle. This worked very effectively both because it generated the commitment of the employees in the plant and, across the site as a whole, had the effect of allaying suspicion among the other trade union representatives.

A different practice emerged within the major seafoods organization. On one of the sites, management were very reluctant to consult with the trade union representatives about the total quality programme. The reason for this was primarily because at the time the programme was being implemented the union representation was relatively weak, although the majority of employees on the plant did belong to the trade union. Management felt that since total quality was essentially an issue for management to implement, there was no need, beyond involving them as employees in the briefing programme, to talk directly to the trade union representatives. This inevitably caused a reaction but we were able to resolve the issue by an early though at times acrimonious meeting with the trade union representatives, briefing them about the programme and reassuring them about some ill-informed fears in relation to redundancy and related issues. The key lesson however was that where there are recognized trade unions, consultation about the total quality programme is important and generates the commitment of the trade union representatives.

In general terms, unless relations are particularly badly strained, it is unlikely that trade union representatives will actively oppose a total quality programme. However, as the TUC guidelines on quality circles indicated, there are wider issues which may result in the trade unions wanting greater involvement in decision making at strategic level. But provided the consultation process on the total quality programme is properly handled in a positive way, then such issues do not usually emerge and most shop stewards at plant level will at least lend their tacit support to the programme.

The first stage of briefing is therefore a general briefing on the overall total quality initiative which provides a strategic briefing of the overall company objectives and sets out a framework for action.

The second stage of the briefing process involves much more specific briefing on how a total quality programme will be implemented at local level and how within different departments and areas of responsibility individuals will become involved in the programme. On the assumption that senior management have already been involved in the strategy development and planning stage of the programme, the detailed briefing is likely to be aimed at middle management, supervision and all employees. As part of the planning process, a detailed briefing pack needs to be prepared.

Set up well in advance and properly planned, the briefing programme should consist of briefings in peer groups. Middle managers who are likely to become involved in interdepartmental task groups, and the supervisors who will work closely with middle management on resolving problems within departments, should be briefed first. This would also enable them to provide the leadership for improvement group or quality circle involvement. It is difficult to generalize how this may be organized, because the size of organizations significantly affects the method of this briefing process, but a number of general principles apply as follows:

● the briefings should be in groups of no more than 25–30, lasting up to about 30 minutes
● the briefings should wherever possible be carried out by a single individual to ensure consistency of message using a standard briefing pack – if an external consultancy has been involved it is best to use the consultants because they are seen as relative neutrals and also as experts in the field. Alternatively the total quality manager can be responsible for this briefing process
● the briefings should be carried out in a concentrated period of time lasting no more than two days – depending on the coverage of employees – to create the maximum impact and ensure that as many people as possible receive the message direct and before rumours can cause any distortion.

The briefings should be introduced by a senior member of management, either the individual responsible for total quality at board level or the total quality manager, particularly if external consultants are being used. This provides evidence of the management commitment and enables some appropriate introduction covering this point to be made at each presentation. The actual presentation should cover the following:

The total quality approach

This should be a statement of the company mission and objectives in establishing the total quality approach. An example of this is:

> To position the company to staff, trade, suppliers and consumers as the leading manufacturer of male fragrances, upper-end mass toiletries/skincare, providing products of outstanding quality, innovation and design.

Definition

This should cover a definition of quality taking account of the company perspectives and priorities. An easy definition of quality is 'an effective system for integrating quality improvement efforts of various groups of the organization so as to provide products and services at levels which allow customer satisfaction'.[1] This definition carries a few useful messages which include:

- an integrated approach which emphasizes the importance of team work and ensures that everybody is involved
- the basic Deming message of continuous improvement
- mention of both products and services, which emphasizes that it is not just the hard product but all aspects of an organization's operations which can be covered, as is also indicated by 'various groups'
- the question of customer satisfaction, which creates the link with the customer – a link often lost in major manufacturing organizations.

Essential features

This should cover some of the key elements in the definition but going into a little more detail:

- total quality is part of the management process of the organization and managed as things go along rather than being controlled after the event – everybody is involved in determining the causes of customer dissatisfaction and aiming for a philosophy of 'right first time' with constant evaluation of cost reductions

- all parts of the business are involved, each operating both as a customer and supplier
- it involves all levels from top to bottom, particularly management, with each level making its own contribution through various problem solving groups
- all stages in the production process are in the provision of services
- it is based on a principle of preventing an error before it occurs
- it is based on continuous measurement and evaluation both within the organization and externally with clients or customers.

The improvement process

The whole approach to total quality is based on the principle of problem prevention, and thus on continuous improvement, as set out in Figure 14.

Figure 14 The Improvement Process

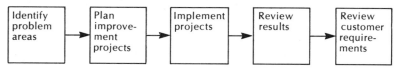

There are two levels involved in the improvement process, the task groups which involve middle managers from various departments and the improvement groups or quality circles which involve office workers or the shop floor. The difference between the two groups is that one looks at interdepartmental problems whereas the others are looking within the immediate area of work. Much of the methodology used in both groups is based on problem solving techniques which are common to both. Critical to the success of a total quality programme is the involvement of the shop floor to generate commitment and interest in the programme. It is therefore important during the briefing sessions to emphasize the role of quality circles within the whole process.

Quality circles are small groups of volunteers working in the same area and meeting regularly to discuss, analyze and solve problems connected with their work under the leadership of a trained section leader or supervisor.

The essential features of quality circles need to be explained in the briefing process in more detail, as follows:

● Although the total quality programme affects everyone in the organization, participation in the quality circles themselves is entirely voluntary. There are no financial rewards for joining and neither are there any penalties. The 'reward' for group members is in reducing day to day frustrations and participating in solving problems within particular departments. I have often found that the voluntary nature is very helpful in promoting the introduction of quality circles because the involvement can be seen as something not forced by the management. When emphasizing the voluntary aspect it is worth saying that there is nothing to lose in participating because the voluntary aspect lasts as long as the quality circle lasts. If at any time the circles are not working satisfactorily it is possible to disband them. Individuals can also walk away from circles at any time. This helps promote a feeling of responsibility and undermines to some extent feelings of cynicism, on the basis that the shop floor and office workers cannot actually lose by joining. Membership of quality circles, particularly in the early stages, is critical and it is sometimes necessary to persuade certain individuals 'behind the scenes' to join in order to ensure that key people have an opportunity to make a contribution. Equally one has to take care that management do not try to manipulate the situation. On one occasion I went to talk to a departmental manager about setting up the group within his area and he produced a list of six people whom he wanted to include and had already 'bent their ear' about it. On further investigation it became apparent that these were people whom he trusted and none of the 'troublemakers' were included in his list. It was finally agreed that the group should be entirely voluntary and not surprisingly his list bore little relationship to the group of people who actually volunteered and successfully participated in a quality circle – much to his surprise!

● They are usually led by an immediate supervisor – if quality circles are part of a total quality programme, which they should be, it is essential that they link into the management process and provide a basis for ensuring problems are resolved and decisions made. Quality circles provide an ideal opportunity, as Deming emphasized, for strengthening the position of supervision and devolving responsibility for quality management to that level. Additionally, the supervisors have an opportunity to shape the group and strengthen their own leadership position. By and large most people accept supervisors as the leaders of quality circles but difficulties sometimes arise where an individual is clearly not suited to playing a leadership role within a circle because of their particular sets of skills. In such situations I have considerable concern about the individual's ability as a supervisor and whether indeed they should be in that position at all. Equally there is often suspicion, particularly within the trade union environment, that the 'imposition' of a supervisor into a quality circle makes it less democratic than they consider it should be. Among office workers there is often not an obvious section head who can lead a group other than a manager who may not be appropriate. On balance the principle should apply that, other than in exceptional circumstances, the supervisor should be leader of the quality circle.

● There should be regular meetings – most quality circles should meet on a regular weekly basis. This means that it can be planned to be at a time which is least disruptive to the work process. For instance it is often found that office quality circles operate best during the middle of the day because the beginning and end of the day tend to be full of major operational pressures. Within production environments the beginning of the shift is often the disruptive period. Whatever the situation, it is important to consult with line management to identify the most appropriate time. In all cases meetings should be restricted to one hour. This discipline is important to give management the confidence that there is some control over the amount of time away from the actual production centre, however important the problem solving activity is. One of the great advantages of the one hour system is that it tends to concentrate the minds of the group members – I have often found that the productivity of quality circle meetings is significantly in excess of an average management meeting. The main reason for the regularity of meetings is to maintain interest and momentum in the problem solving process. However there are occasions when it is not possible to have regular weekly meetings – for instance, when sales staff are involved – and then the meetings can be arranged in a more flexible way.

● Five to ten members usually make up a quality circle, and although this is not inflexible, it reflects the fact that with less than four members it can be difficult to get a group working well together, as personalities may intrude; and with more than ten people, particularly where there is only one hour available for the meeting, it is extremely difficult to involve all members in the group. If there are more volunteers than there are places within the group, as can happen in large departments, the best way to ensure group members are 'selected', without causing suspicion, is to ask the department as a whole to decide among themselves who will be a member of the group. It is possible to rotate membership of the group over a period of time, probably once every six months to allow sufficient momentum on the problem solving activity to be built up. Certainly changes should not occur while a project is being carried out.

● Members usually select which problems to tackle themselves – obviously within the overall umbrella of the total quality programme. The main criteria for problem selection are that the members are unable to tackle and resolve the problems themselves, and that the problems exclude, as might be expected, anything relating to terms and conditions of employment. This aspect of quality circles often causes considerable concern among management, who fear they may lose control of the process. However, I have found that provided common sense applies and people are reminded that they can only deal with problems that they can resolve, difficulties have seldom arisen and if they have, the group members themselves have excluded problems which are too difficult or unacceptable. The usual pattern is that the early problems to be identified and resolved tend to be fairly simple. Certainly I would always encourage groups to try to gain momentum before moving on to the more complex problems requiring a longer time to solve – bearing in mind the one hour a week principle. I have also found that in trade union environments it is clearly understood that pay and conditions are outside the remit of quality circles. In non-union environments there is sometimes a tendency to try to use quality circles as a means of raising pay and conditions issues where no other forum exists. This is not a serious matter but clearly if issues of this nature arise it reflects the fact that there is a problem to which management should at least respond. The problem selection process is also important because quality circle methodology provides for problem solving to be carried out on a project basis – in other words, one problem is dealt with at a time, and the concentration is on actually obtaining solutions.

● There should be systematic analysis of problems – the principle of quality circles which also extends to task groups is that problem solving is carried out in a systematic way using a number of relatively simple techniques. Details of the techniques are discussed on pages 117–48. Much of the training involved in introducing a total quality programme and the consequent task groups and quality circles is based on systematic problem solving. This approach helps groups to approach and solve problems in a step by step way and ensures as far as possible that when solutions are reached they have been properly researched and obtained through a logical process. There is often concern among management that some of the solutions that are put forward may be ill considered, superficial or impractical. The problem solving approach tends to eliminate the likelihood of this and it is rare for quality circle solutions to be rejected by management for these reasons. They can of course be rejected for other reasons.

● The presentation of the results – once a group has completed a project, which on average tends to take between eight and ten meetings depending on the complexity of the problem, they present their solution to management in a way that enables managers to understand how the problem was identified, what the proposed solution is and what action is necessary to implement the solution. The presentation process provides an excellent opportunity for communication between management and quality circles, representing as they do the shop floor, and often creates an evironment of much better understanding of why things happen in an organization. It is also important that proposals are presented to the level of management which has the authority to agree changes, so that a fairly rapid decision can be made on the implementation of a particular proposal. The system of presenting results gives confidence to management that they do have some control over the process and they have effectively a right of veto. Equally it is important that management respond quickly to proposals either in agreeing that implementation should take place or, if deciding to reject a particular set of proposals, ensuring that this is properly explained and that alternatives are put forward. One of the difficulties often encountered at this stage in the process is that management can be slow to respond for perfectly good operating reasons and within a timetable which would be normal to them. This causes frustration and disillusionment at shop floor level and therefore it is important that the momentum is maintained by rapid response or by explanations if delays do occur.

● The quality circles implement their own proposals – once management have agreed a set of proposals the quality circles are responsible for implementation, subject of course to any detailed technical work that may be required. Certainly the circles are responsible for communicating the proposed changes to all levels, ensuring that there is commitment to make the changes. Clearly if a new process is being introduced as a result of quality circle proposals, problems of implementation will be considerable if they do not explain to their peers why the changes are taking place. The impact of this communication can be considerable. I remember on one occasion within a seafoods organization a circle presenting their proposals to their colleagues for some small redesign of the line layout which would improve the quality control and at the same time make the tasks simpler to carry out. While there was full agreement that the proposals should be introduced, the fact that their peers were able to stand up and make a presentation to a relatively large group of people made the greatest impact and probably generated greater commitment to the total quality programme than any other feature, particularly since it was clearly supported by management who showed commitment through the rapid support for implementation. Many solutions require technical input and in particular, on production lines, engineering support which is outside the scope of the quality circle. All engineering departments have schedules of work and it may be that they are unable to respond quickly to making technical engineering changes in accordance with the quality circle proposals. If this is the case, management must communicate possible delays or consider rescheduling the engineering work to ensure that the momentum for change is maintained.

Benefits

The briefing pack not only needs to explain what total quality is about and how individuals may become involved but also needs to sell in the programme. The particular benefits of a total quality programme which require consideration include:

- increasing the performance and profitability of the organization by getting things 'right first time'
- creating a process of business improvement
- giving those actually doing the job more opportunity to use their experience and know-how
- providing a means for tapping knowledge of all employees
- improving both productivity and quality
- winning commitment to the organization and improving employee relations
- improving customer satisfaction.

The overall advantages of the total quality programme can be summarized in the following diagram:

Figure 15 Benefits of Total Quality

Company	Everybody benefits	Employees
● Improved quality		● Job satisfaction
● Improved productivity		● Participation
● Reduced costs		● Training
● Better relationships		● Status/Recognition

Including the customer!

The programme

The final part of the briefing should provide a broad outline of the timetable involved in the implementation programme. In particular it should emphasize:

(a) the briefing process explaining how everyone in the organization is going to receive a briefing to enable them to understand the main elements of the total quality programme, their contribution to the programme and their possible participation in a number of activities;

(b) the training programmes which would involve the leaders of the task groups and the quality circles in a number of 'off the job' training programmes. There would also be shorter training programmes for all employees covering some of the basic techniques involved in problem solving and some simple statistical techniques. The actual timing of the training course should be given to enable those who will be attending to organize their affairs to allow their release and to demonstrate commitment;

(c) the implementation phase which is centred on the launch of both the task groups and the quality circles with possible dates being given and emphasis being placed on the need to seek volunteers for membership of such groups. Explanations should be given as to how the volunteers should let it be known that they wish to participate and what will happen if there are too many volunteers;

(d) the review phase which includes monitoring the progress of the programme and in particular emphasizes the concept of continuous improvement, whereby throughout the overall process there will be continuous review, change and development to ensure ongoing success.

At the end of the briefing process, the overall launch of the total quality programme and detailed face to face meetings, there should be little doubt within the organization that management are determined to make changes. There inevitably will be cynicism and comments and therefore the momentum needs to be maintained. Face to face meetings at least create a situation where cynicism begins to break down as action takes over. The other advantage of the face to face briefings is that there is always the opportunity for people to ask questions and, although quite often questions tend to be simplistic, it often gives the external consultant or the total quality manager a good understanding of the hopes and fears of everybody concerned.

I have often met resistance by management to such an all embracing approach to the implementation of a total quality programme particularly if that type of communication is unusual within the organization concerned. Resistance comes mainly because there is clearly disruption to production. On the whole the extent of this disruption depends on the technology involved and the ability to provide cover while production continues. Within offices it is unlikely that there will be any direct loss of efficiency. The cost of any loss is likely to be negligible compared to the likely impact of a successful total quality programme. The Crosby analysis of costs indicates that typically a company which is operating at the 'uncertainty' level is incurring quality costs of up to 20 per cent of revenue with the possibility of this being reduced progressively to under five per cent of revenue. If one accepts this analysis, then the loss of a few hours production is unlikely to prove a significant problem. What is much more important is that if one accepts the analysis of all those who have been involved in total quality, including Deming, Juran, Crosby and others, that quality is about attitudes, then these have to be tackled head on. The only way this can be done is by face to face communication to ensure that everybody at least understands the message – even if they don't initially accept it. Provided action follows then the beginning of changes in attitude can take place.

Chapter 12
OPERATING ELEMENTS – TRAINING

In Chapter 8 I have already identified that there are a number of different training events which need to take place covering:

- top management
- management
- task group leaders/quality circle leaders
- facilitators.

Much of the training provided at all these levels is central to the introduction of total quality but it needs to be adapted to ensure that the training needs for each level are appropriately met. Here we consider the different aspects of training under the following headings:

- concepts of quality
- interpersonal skills
- techniques.

Concepts of quality

The purpose of training in concepts of quality is to ensure that there is a thorough understanding within the organization both of quality and the specific company objectives. In introducing total quality it should be emphasized that it consists of:

- a philosophy of getting things 'right first time' or 'zero defects'
- a systematic approach to improving the overall quality performance of the company based on a body of principles and methods
- a central strategy to the company based on an integrated system involving all processes and all people
- a focus on customer requirements.

In explaining the approach to total quality it is important to emphasize the particular focus of the strategy. For instance, a number of alternative strategies can be considered where the emphasis may be on:

- increasing efficiency and productivity
- creating a better product or service
- improving performance of people within the organization
- getting the most out of the existing organizational structure
- transforming work processes
- maximizing customer satisfaction.

During the training process it is important for top management to focus on their particular objectives and review this on a continuous basis.

It is also useful to pick up on some of the principles addressed by Deming, Juran and Crosby to give a focus to the organization's total quality strategy. This provides an opportunity to contrast it with the existing quality control approach within an organization, which is likely to be characterized by:

- controlling quality after the event – in other words quality control based on inspection
- a cost to the business which is considered almost as an inevitable part of the business process
- the responsibility being primarily that of production with none of the functional services involved in the process
- little emphasis on causes of problems but concentration on effects characterized by the philosophy of 'inspecting in' quality
- a mythology about the inability to improve performance beyond certain levels which are accepted as inevitable
- little true evaluation of the cost of quality on an integrated basis – with cost measured often only in the quality control department (ie inspectors) and possibly as the specific costs arising out of complaints.

As Deming so clearly demonstrated, that philosophy is very much centred on 'the customers get what they pay for' and the higher the quality standard the greater the cost. In contrast the total quality approach should be based on the principle that the customer determines the level of quality and service which is required. This is then provided in a cost effective manner. To achieve this the total quality approach is characterized by:

- real time management of performance whereby each person has responsibility for ensuring they meet the highest quality standards as they do the job, not assuming that someone else will correct defects or problems
- an inbuilt principle of getting things right first time on the basis that 'if you can measure it, you can repair it'
- involvement of everybody within the business in achieving quality standards
- constant emphasis on improvement and cost reductions.

This approach provides a framework whereby one can emphasize that total quality can only exist within a dynamic and motivated organization continually setting itself new standards of performance. Within this framework it is possible to introduce some basic principles of quality in relation to existing performance by demonstrating first that quality costs are broadly divided into four categories (prevention, appraisal, internal failure and external failure costs) and that the reasons for poor quality performance can be divided into assignable causes and random variations (see Chapter 9).

The purpose of this part of any training programme which is likely to apply to all levels is to ensure a broad understanding that:

- total quality is something different from the traditional approaches
- the costs of quality involve every aspect of the organization's operation
- there are ways of measuring the costs of quality which go beyond the traditional simplistic costs of failure
- quality can be controlled either by identifying directly reasons for problems (assignable causes) or by controlling random variations.

Once the basic concepts have been introduced to a group they need to identify for themselves quality issues within their areas of responsibility and within the company as a whole. At this early stage within a course programme I found that a useful way forward is to ask the group to brainstorm all the quality issues they see within the organization and for these then to be grouped together, however unscientifically at this stage, under assignable causes and random variations. This provides a framework for discussion during the course programme and begins to focus people's minds on the issues within the organization. In addition the initial brainstorm list should be divided under two main headings to broaden the scope of the discussion as follows:

- factors in your organization that are likely to help a successful approach to total quality
- factors in your organization that are likely to hinder the introduction of a total quality approach.

An example of the importance of using this approach was shown within one organization where during the brainstorm it was identified that one of the possible hindrances to introduction was the trade union. Senior management had already advised me that it was unlikely that the trade union would cause any problems and yet the group of circle leaders who were involved in the training programme clearly identified this as a major issue. As a result we were able to hold discussions with the trade unions and resolve a number of difficulties without detracting from the implementation programme.

Interpersonal skills

The introduction of a total quality programme within an organization is based on the principle that all those within the organization will work effectively together to resolve quality issues and improve the performance of the organization. This is mainly achieved by introducing the concept of task groups and quality circles as the basis for problem solving groups. Many people within the organization would not have previously been used to working in groups to solve problems, and therefore a number of basic training needs can be identified – in particular the need to develop:

- group leadership skills
- group working skills
- communication and presentation skills.

While a great deal of benefit can be derived within a total quality programme from improving the interpersonal skills of management and the work force in these areas, I do not consider that primary level training in these skills is essential. In all cases the training should be seen as a means to an end – effective problem solving within the total quality environment. As a result I have found that in developing training programmes it is important to ensure that the programmes are action oriented and 'hands on' and that much of the learning takes place through actually doing rather than providing a great deal of input on the theoretical side. The approach therefore should be largely pragmatic and results oriented.

Group leadership skills

A good starting point in introducing the concept of group leading skills as part of a total quality programme is to identify exactly what a group leader is likely to be asked to do. In other words, clearly identify the training needs by analyzing the role. Group leaders are likely to operate at two levels, the task group leaders, who are likely to be leaders of the middle management task groups and will often be the peers of those in the group, and quality circle leaders, who will usually but not exclusively be the supervisors, who are also taking responsibility for quality circles. In both cases the role of the group leaders is likely to involve:

- communicating about total quality and the work of the group throughout the area of responsibility
- seeking members for the group and, in the case of quality circles, volunteers
- chairing meetings and providing leadership
- developing the skills of the group members and allocating tasks
- making practical arrangements for the meeting
- ensuring there is provision for specialist help to assist the deliberations of the group.

In order to enable the group leader to fulfil these tasks, such leaders will probably need to be:

- good organizers
- enthusiastic
- good decision-makers

- good with people
- patient
- good at listening
- fair
- good communicators
- full of initiative
- good team players.

By introducing these concepts early into a training programme I have then asked the members of the training programme to score the performance of the leaders on the so-called leadership profile (see Figure 16). The methodology is simple and pragmatic. At the end of each problem solving activity within the training programme the nominated leader of the group scores him/herself as an individual while the group as a whole separately assesses the performance of that leader. Comparisons are then made between the scores and discussions take place on both the strengths and weaknesses which are identified jointly and also on any significant differences in score or perception between the group and the individuals.

Figure 16 Leadership Profile

Name _____

	Good	Above average	Average	Below average	Poor
Good organizer					
Enthusiastic					
Can make decisions					
Good with people					
Patient					
Good at listening					
Fair					
Good communicator					
Has initiative					
Good team person					

The trainer needs to counsel and discuss issues with each individual and the process is repeated throughout the training course so that each individual has an opportunity to be scored on their performance. It is unusual for people to be concerned about this approach because at the end of the day good sense and objectivity tend to prevail because everybody is going to go through the process. I have also found that inevitably the scoring and objectivity tends to get more effective as a training course unfolds with a tendency for better scores to be achieved early on in the programme and as people understand the criteria tougher marking begins to develop.

Since the primary role of group leaders is to run an effective meeting, it is also necessary to provide some basic input into how to run an effective meeting. Again a relatively simplistic approach is necessary which can then be measured and at the same time improved as individual leaders develop. The basic approach should include:

- plan the meeting by making clear, either by the use of an agenda or some other technique, what the objective of the particular meeting should be and what results are likely to come out of the meeting. This can be achieved by the leader outlining at the beginning of the meeting exactly where (s)he would like to get to by the end of the meeting
- keep to the plan
- keep control – although it should be remembered that total quality is a participative process
- encourage all to contribute by ensuring that even the quieter members of the group are actually given the 'space' to make their contribution. Quite often it is the quieter group members who will make effective contributions if given the opportunity
- motivate and praise
- delegate the various activities within the group such as somebody to take notes, somebody to seek information before a meeting or make a particular contact and ensure that the leader does not end up doing everything
- take notes – I remember on one occasion in a quality circle in a major Japanese firm they sought specialist technical help in looking at the cost options for providing a shunter lorry within the warehouse complex. The transport manager came to the

meeting to provide such data and went through it in a great deal of detail. No single member of the group, including the leader, took notes and of course there was some embarrassment when this was realized at the end of the meeting

● summarize at the end of the meeting to ensure that all agree what has been achieved or what is to be done. It is useful also to summarize various strategic points of the meeting to ensure that all are committed to the ideas and progress made

● plan ahead by ensuring, if necessary by using the activity report, that it is clear to all group members what needs to take place before the next meeting and what is likely to be done at the next meeting. Additionally I found that it is useful to have a broad project plan which is flexible but at the same time provides a framework within which a group can work to give it direction.

Leadership training within a total quality environment is aimed primarily at ensuring that group leaders are capable of running effective groups and concentrates on two aspects – the leadership skills required by using a simple profile which is regularly measured during a training programme (and of course can be used as a measure afterwards) and giving structure to meetings. Within this framework the key to success is practice and individual counselling, an environment which is primarily supportive.

Group working skills

As in the case of leadership skills, the approach to introducing effective group working as part of total quality training should be essentially pragmatic and low key and should not introduce a major theoretical framework. It is important to explain that to be effective and constructive a meeting needs a certain amount of self-discipline, not just in preparing contributions beforehand but also in controlling feelings so that disagreements can be dealt with on the basis of logic not emotion.

The basic rules that individuals should adopt in approaching meetings include:

● listen to what other people are actually saying in detail. Even if individuals are sympathetic to the ideas being expressed by other people, they can often switch off if they feel they have a general sense of what is being said. This often means that something vital can be missed and it becomes difficult to support or indeed refute an argument later if one has to go back over the same ground again

● participate – it is irresponsible to 'opt out' in a meeting and let other people do all the work. At the same time if one disagrees violently, which can often result in opting out from what is being said, it is a specific responsibility to make one's view heard

● be consistent and objective by putting forward arguments in a logical way, trying not to let personal feelings come to the fore

● ask questions as appropriate in order to clarify other people's contributions. It also demonstrates that one is listening to the contributions of others and responding in a positive way

● summarize what one thinks has been said, asking whether it is properly understood in order to try to help group members who are not putting across their ideas clearly

● involve the quieter group members and do not necessarily rely on the group leader to do this by asking them directly for a contribution

● avoid emotional argument

● avoid side issues

● co-operate with the group leader – this may seem an obvious point but it is easy for a group to disrupt a meeting if they do not wish to co-operate with the group leader.

One of the most effective ways of demonstrating how groups can work well together (or not, as the case may be) is by using a problem solving exercise which compares individual performance with group performance. There are many examples of this type of exercise but one good example is the so-called 'desert survival' which asks a group of people to compare their individual ranking of a list of priority items with the team ranking, and then comparing both sets of scores with the scores of the so-called experts. In general the difference between the individual ranking and the expert ranking is greater than the difference between the group ranking and the expert ranking. Figure 17 demonstrates how this can be done. This is often a powerful tool and demonstrates simply but effectively the power of group work and at the same time gives the opportunity during a training programme to illustrate group working issues such as those outlined above.

Figure 17 The Desert Survival Exercise

Item	STEP 1 Your Individual Ranking	STEP 2 The Team Ranking	STEP 3 Survival Experts Ranking	STEP 4 Difference Between Steps 1 & 3	STEP 5 Difference Between Steps 2 & 3
1 quart of water per person					
Jack-knife					
A pair of sunglasses per person					
A book entitled 'Edible Animals of the Desert'					
Bottle of salt tablets (1,000 tablets)					
Cosmetic mirror					
Flashlight (4 battery size)					
Magnetic compass					
Compress kit with gauze					
2 quarts 180 proof vodka					
.45 caliber pistol (loaded)					
Parachute (red and white)					
Sectional air map of the area					
1 top coat per person					
Plastic raincoat (large size)					
TOTALS the lower the better				Individual Score Step 4	Team Score Step 5

Source: *Human Synergistics: Verax* (1974)

Figure 18 Problem Solving Form

GROUP: _____ LEADER: _____ Date: _____

Definition of Problem _____

Date started: _____ Date Completed: _____
List of Causes: _____

Analysis of Causes: _____

Description of Data Collection Procedures/Summary: _____

List of Alternative Solutions: _____

Recommended Plan of Action: _____

Date of Management Presentation: _____ Approval: ___YES ____NO
Expected Implementation Date: _____

Expected Results:	Actual Results:

Communication and presentation skills

All problem solving activities associated with a total quality programme within an organization are based on achieving commitment to change and actually implementing that change quickly and effectively. In order to achieve this it is necessary to communicate with the decision makers in order to get their agreement to changes and also with everybody else directly affected by the changes in order to ensure they understand what is required of them and that they are committed to those changes. Communication therefore becomes central to the whole process, particularly for those people in middle management, supervision and the grades below.

Once a project is completed it needs to be presented to the decision makers for authorization, to other departments/specialists for action and operation and to those directly affected for their commitment. Presentations are normally quite formal and should cover the following:

- clear identification of the problem
- the proposed solution
- the benefits to be gained from the changes proposed
- the costs of any changes offset against any financial benefits
- method of implementation
- how the results will be monitored
- action required from those attending the presentation.

At the end of the presentation the key points should be entered on a 'problem solving' form so there is a formal record (see Figure 18).

In helping people to prepare for presentations and learn the basics of making presentations the following approach can be helpful:

- structure – it is important to have a clear *beginning* which has a statement of what is going to be covered during the talk, a *middle* where the facts or messages which need to be put across are logically presented and finally an *end* with a brief summary and/or what action is required
- be natural – despite the obvious nerves which often creep into presentations being given by more junior members of staff, every effort should be made not to become stilted or unnatural

- show enthusiasm – people should demonstrate their commitment to the proposals by putting them across in a positive way; again nerves can lead to stilted monologues which convey a lack of commitment
- use everyday language – shop floor workers in particular have a tendency to assume that they should adopt some more sophisticated and technical language in making their presentations. This is not the case and presentations are often more effective if they are put forward in a simple and clear way
- maintain audience contact – by directly watching the audience, maintaining eye contact and watching for reaction, positive and negative, to what is being said
- be audible
- go at the right speed – avoid in particular the tendency to 'gabble'. People should not be afraid to use pauses to allow the audience to assimilate what has been said
- avoid distracting mannerisms

This basic checklist of eight key points for effective presentations provides a framework not only for individuals unfamiliar with public speaking but also, in a fairly noncontentious way, provides a framework for the trainer to help individuals develop. As in the other parts of the training programme the key to learning is to ensure during the training programmes that everybody concerned has an opportunity to make presentations and to receive feedback on how they have been performing against this type of checklist. Within a training programme this can be done easily in a non-threatening environment to enable people to develop at their own pace.

Over many years of running total quality programmes there have been very, very few exceptions where people have not had the confidence after training and practice to get up and make presentations to more senior people. The effect on personal development, confidence and commitment is often dramatic. Additionally it provides a powerful tool in demonstrating to top management the talent that is available at lower levels within the organization. Perhaps the most outstanding example of this was within the major seafoods organization. After the total quality programme had been running some twelve months it was decided to reinforce top management commitment and at the same time provide evidence of progress by arranging a meeting between the board of the company and the task group and quality circle leaders. The meeting was held near one of the factory sites and it was noted that for the first time a board meeting had been held away from headquarters in London. The meeting consisted of a series of presentations from the group leaders to the board of the company, including the chairman. The fact that junior management, supervision and shop floor employees presented their ideas and solutions to top managment had a dramatic impact on all those involved. The top management recognized the importance of continuing their commitment to the total quality programme and for the first time, perhaps, recognized the talent that was available throughout the organization. For the junior members of staff, who were meeting many of the board members for the first time, there was the recognition that after all top management were 'as human as us' and really were committed to the total quality programme. Much of the training and impetus for such effective presentations was based on the simple concepts outlined above. This basic approach has the advantage of making the training quick and effective and at the same time concentrating on the key factor – successful implementation – rather than providing extensive training in all aspects of interpersonal skills.

In summary interpersonal skills training within the context of total quality requires three basic elements:

● group leadership skills
● skills for working in groups
● communication and presentation skills.

For top management and probably for senior and middle management there are also requirements for understanding and developing management style and effective management in the broadest sense. These are basic requirements which should apply within any organization and in themselves do not form part of a total quality programme. Nevertheless it should be borne in mind that weaknesses in management may require rectification. Improvement in management and management style may be necessary. This is likely to be identified during the diagnostic stage and a specific training and development programme can be put together to meet any identified needs. In particular changes in management style may be required as part of the development of participative management associated with the total quality approach. It is important however to distinguish between the specific requirements of total quality training, outlined here, and broader management training requirements which are a wider issue and which I do not intend to cover within this context.

Techniques

There is a tendency among many total quality practitioners to allow the techniques associated with total quality to become more and more sophisticated and more mathematical. This can have the effect of not only turning people off but actually diluting the basic message which is associated with significant changes in attitude. The Japanese success in introducing statistical process control throughout all levels of the organization over a 30–40 year period must be seen in the context of a process which began to be introduced into Japan in the early 1950s. It started with top management and progressed through to supervision by the early 1960s. From that time it was progressively extended on to the shop floor and across all disciplines, and at the same time was mirrored by developments at Japan's universities and schools, where the basic statistical techniques are taught. This environment, which allows for an understanding of statistical tools on a national basis, is a far cry from the environment within the UK and Europe. There is evidence within Europe that the concept of quality and some of the associated techniques are beginning to percolate through the school system. There is little evidence of this at the present time within the UK. In this environment it is important that within an organization introducing total quality, simple and straightforward techniques are taught to achieve maximum results in problem solving. Certainly it is my view that for most people within an organization it is sufficient to create a problem solving environment with some basic tools and techniques to achieve remarkable results, although it may be necessary at a higher level to introduce more sophisticated techniques.

Joint problem solving

The key to success in introducing total quality within an organization, involving task groups and quality circles in seeking ways of continuous improvement to quality, is based on a systematic approach to joint problem solving. While details often vary, the principles are based on:

● depersonalizing conflicts by diluting emotions and adopting a systematic approach
● providing a logical framework which encourages the facts to come to the surface so that the facts rather than the individuals determine the solution
● integrating the objectives of the organization and of the people working in it.

To achieve this an action-oriented problem solving process can be used as set out in Figure 19 with the following main components:

● problem identification – using brainstorming (see page 106), a full list of current operating problems including quality problems should be identified. In selecting a project to work on, groups should take account of factors such as:
   – is the problem in their own area?
   – does it affect the whole group?
   – does it occur frequently?
   – will it save manhours and time?
   – will it improve quality – reduce waste?
   – does it cause frustration and consequent inefficiency?
   – is it within the competency of the group to resolve?
● establish a goal – this should be a target for improvement for the specific project, such as a reduction to a certain level of rejects or an increase in productivity by a certain amount. In all cases it should be measurable but at the same time should not become encased in concrete and immovable. On the principle of continuous improvement, whatever goal is set needs to be reviewed continuously. The importance of setting a goal is that it provides a basis for focusing the group's activity and establishing whether success has been achieved.
● prioritize and plan – this should provide an indication to the group of the priorities in achieving a goal and the plan of action which is developed in order to enable them to achieve it. For instance, it is important to establish what data needs to be collected, when it should be collected and, broadly speaking, the point at which it is anticipated that a solution may be found

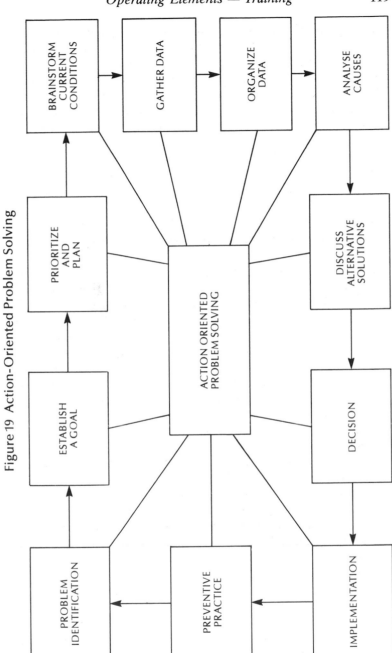

Figure 19 Action-Oriented Problem Solving

- brainstorm the current conditions and likely causes of particular problems – this provides a list of all areas that may need investigation in the problem-solving activity
- gather statistical data – in most cases it will be necessary to set up procedures to gather data, which can be done in a simplistic way. It may also be useful and necessary to access historical data or use existing systems – such as laboratory test results or records of yield – to provide a thorough understanding of the likely causes of a particular problem
- organize the data – by using charts, diagrams or other means to present the data in a carefully structured way so that it can be analyzed in detail
- analyze causes – in order to determine the most dominant cause of a particular problem and also to try to get underneath the more obvious symptoms to verify the true cause
- discuss alternative solutions – having analyzed in depth the actual causes it is likely that more than one solution needs consideration. Certainly in establishing credibility in problem-solving activity, it is important to demonstrate that alternative solutions have been discussed before a particular solution has been identified as the most appropriate. In discussing alternative solutions, consideration must also be given to the goal which has already been set because the criteria for solutions will determine the most appropriate solution. For instance, a solution which is looking to reduce costs may be different from a solution which is looking to improve productivity
- make the decision – having considered alternative solutions, a particular recommendation is now made to solve the problem and put forward to management for approval
- implement – one of the failings of problem solving activity is that in the euphoria of having resolved a complex problem, groups often fail to include in their solution a detailed action plan showing the timetable and responsibility for implementation
- use preventive practice – this should be based on the principle of monitoring progress against the likely results which have been predicted using appropriate statistical techniques. It is unlikely that a perfect solution will be found at the first attempt and as part of the philosophy of continuous improve-

● ment it is necessary to monitor progress and adjust the solution to ensure further improvement. Again I have found that this part of the total quality programme can often be difficult to implement, especially in an organization where the underlying culture has in the past been that once a problem is solved, it has 'gone away'. Successful total quality programmes must be based on continuous adjustment and review so that the whole cycle of the action-oriented problemsolving process is continuously repeated over a prolonged period of time.

One of the keys to successful joint problem solving is to ensure that discussions are carried out in an organized and controlled way in order to achieve specific results. A useful checklist to use when managing the problem solving activity includes the following key points:

● state the problem NOT the answer – there is a great tendency for people, particularly those inexperienced in problem solving, to immediately jump into the answer stage without fully analyzing what exactly the problem is. A classic example of this was within one task group among a group of salesmen who were reviewing, they thought, the checklist they used when approaching new clients. During the course of the discussion it became apparent that different checklists were in fact being used. It had been thought the answer was to review the checklist, but in fact the real problem was that different checklists were being used

● establish key facts – it is critical to do this using whatever techniques are necessary

● restate the problem – having established the key facts it may be necessary to redefine the problem. There is a great tendency in many organizations to make decisions on the basis of the symptoms rather than on the causes – in other words not concentrating on the key facts. The most obvious example of this which we encounter daily is failure to identify exactly what the customer requires, thinking that high quality means as Crosby said 'luxurious' without recognizing that people are prepared to accept the highest quality standard based on their definition of what their specific requirement is, which may be expensive or cheap

- identify possible obstacles – this is an important part of problem solving activity because by doing so it may be possible either to identify a solution or often to redirect efforts from a situation where the obstacles appear to be insurmountable or are within the responsibility of other parties. In one total quality programme, a group of engineers identified that the major problem on the particular site was the lack of investment in equipment and that many of the engineering problems could be resolved by wholesale reinvestment. This was too big an obstacle to overcome because it required investment decisions at the highest level within the organization. On the other hand, having recognized that this was an obstacle and put it on one side, the engineers were able to come up with a series of lower level changes which had a radical effect on the productivity of the plant in question
- list possible ways of overcoming obstacles – using brainstorming again it is useful to consider every possible idea that would help to overcome any of the obstacles. Quite often, although this needs to be handled carefully, obstacles are identified as being attitudes of groups of people or particular individuals. How often does one hear on a plant from production workers that the biggest problem is the attitude of the engineer who is not willing to listen to their views?
- establish criteria – this involves deciding the yardsticks against which possible solutions may be measured while at the same time helping to keep the discussions on an objective level. Possible criteria may include acceptability to particular groups, cost, time limits, ease of implementation and effectiveness
- discuss solutions against criteria – this provides an opportunity to narrow down the range of alternatives until the most practical emerge, by comparing the possible solutions against the criteria that have been established
- agree an action plan – at any stage in the problem solving activity it is important to agree who does what, when and what form of feedback is necessary.

With this structure it is possible to achieve hard results and at the same time show the decision makers and all those affected that a detailed analysis has been made of each problem. There is nothing special or unique about the approach but it requires discipline. The approach also requires all those involved to use questioning techniques which can often provoke ideas and responses during group discussions. Some examples of these include:

● direct question – usually requiring a yes or no answer – its use is limited but provides a clear cut result
● leading question – which gives alternative choices but points in a particular direction, for instance 'Wouldn't you agree that the solution to this problem must be the introduction of better measuring equipment?'
● factual question – this requires a definitive answer, for instance 'How many defectives did we have during the last six week period?'
● overhead question – this calls for some kind of explanation, for instance 'What would you do with the paperwork?'
● redirected question – this maintains the participation and involvement of the group, for instance, 'John wondered whether the solution to this problem would be another inspector, what do you think, Mary?'

Within the overall framework described above it is important to introduce a number of other detailed techniques which provide the tools to help systematic problem solving to operate effectively.

Brainstorming

Brainstorming is a way of getting as many ideas as possible on a problem or a solution in the shortest possible time. Brainstorming works most effectively when there is a group of people responding within the following framework:

● don't discuss – just concentrate on writing up ideas as quickly as possible without criticizing anything that is said
● build on others' suggestions – by using the thoughts of others to trigger one's own thought processes – the classic lateral thinking approach
● go for quantity – by trying to write up as many ideas as possible within a period of time, say five or ten minutes
● be imaginative – quite often the most creative solutions come from initially daft ideas; avoid creating an environment where

people are inhibited from putting forward ideas because others criticize or laugh at them.

After this process it is possible to go through the list and edit out anything that is inappropriate.

Brainstorming is a critical part of all problem solving activities and is used both at the problem identification stage as well as in the various problem solving and creative stages of the process. It is a technique which is often underrated and which people become better at the more they use it. It is based on the principle that discussion can be helpful not only in solving problems but in changing attitudes, obtaining commitment and, perhaps most important, in developing ideas.

Data collection

Analysis of quality problems in order to determine solutions needs to be based on data collected on quality performance whether it be simple, such as the number of rejects and the reason for the rejects on a particular line, or a more complex cost analysis. The process of collecting data is based first on brainstorming a list of all the factors likely to contribute to a particular situation. For instance, in Figure 20 there is a list of seven major reasons for customer complaints within an organization. Information was collected over an eight-week period indicating the number of complaints and the cost of those complaints based on its type, as indicated in the figure. A similar approach can be used for the collection of data on number of rejects and reasons for them, doing this in a systematic way by observation, reference to historical data, reference to a particular department (eg finance) or any other appropriate method.

Methods of analysis

Once all the data has been collected, it needs to be analyzed so that it is possible to identify the most important causes of a problem or the key features of a particular situation. The most commonly used method where figures are available is Pareto analysis.

Pareto analysis is named after the Italian economist Vilfredo Pareto, who in 1897 investigated the distribution of wealth and

Figure 20 Analysis of Customer Complaints

COMPLAINT	Weeks	1	2	3	4	5	6	7	8
				Number of complaints/Repair costs (£100s)					
Order wrongly addressed		1/3	3/9	7/17	2/6	9/29	1/2	–	2/7
Order incomplete		21/26	26/52	18/64	12/32	9/28	27/96	3/9	16/52
Order date		4/0	1/3	–	–	3/10	–	–	6/19
Order faulty		45/136	63/191	29/54	72/217	81/283	35/106	51/158	43/109
Wrong order		5/18	2/6	4/13	9/32	3/10	6/20	7/25	1/3
Didn't arrive		12/39	10/29	36/116	21/56	29/102	5/14	7/21	26/84
Not what the customer expected		12/37	9/27	7/24	3/81	14/44	7/24	9/27	11/36

income in Italy and discovered that a very large percentage of both were in the hands of a very small percentage of the population. Applying the same principles in various fields of business, it has often been found that typically:

- 80 per cent of sales revenue is earned by 20 per cent of the firm's products
- 20 per cent of the items in a factory store may account for 80 per cent of the volume of items issued
- 80 per cent of defects are caused by 20 per cent of the possible defect types.

Pareto analysis is therefore no more than a simple system to identify the 'vital few and trivial many' causes of particular problems based on the principle that 20 per cent of the problems cause 80 per cent of the trouble. Using the information about customer complaints collected in Figure 20, it is possible to carry out a Pareto analysis to identify the vital few facts about customer complaints in the eight week period analyzed. As can be seen in Figure 21 the analysis shows that three categories of the complaints (the vital few) accounted for 80 per cent of all complaints. This can be more clearly shown on the histogram in Figure 22. In carrying out a Pareto analysis it is always best to present the figures on a percentage basis which is easier for those listening to the presentation to assimilate than a mass of figures. In addition presentation in histogram form provides a visual demonstration of the problems and leaves little doubt as to the situation. One other feature which is demonstrated by the example illustrated is that it is possible to

Figure 21 Percentage Analysis of Complaints

Complaint	Percentage of Complaints	Cumulative Percentage
Order faulty	48%	48%
Didn't arrive	17.8%	65.8%
Order incomplete	13.8%	79.6%
Other	20.4%	100%

Figure 22 Pareto Analysis of Complaints

% of all complaints

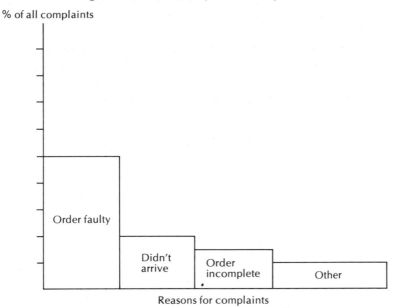

Reasons for complaints

collect the data in more than one way, ie. numbers and cost. In the situation described there was a relatively close correlation between the number and the total costs of the various complaints. This may not always be the case and as a result may require two different analyses. Pareto analysis enables one to highlight key issues and direct the priorities of a particular project. However data needs to be readily available to collect and to be analyzed.

Such data may not always be available. For instance, a group may be looking at the problem of duplicate orders in an order processing area and the issue is to consider the causes of this. Alternatively a group may be looking at the reasons for poor communication in any particular area. In both cases it is not possible (or useful) to collect hard data on the situation. How does one prioritize the likely causes of a problem when faced with this?

One method which I have found useful is taken from job evaluation techniques – paired comparisons. Paired comparisons is a method of establishing priorities from a list of possible causes of a problem by comparing each cause 'in pairs'. Scoring is allocated on the basis that the most important problem scores two points, if two problems are of broadly similar importance score one point each and a problem which is of less importance scores nothing. By totalling up the scores a rank order is produced (as shown in Figure 23). This lists a number of factors which a group had considered could be causing the communication problem and had then gone on to carry out a paired comparison to arrive at a ranking. The method is quick and simple and involves a high level of participation which means that the results tend to be easily accepted. The

Figure 23 The Paired Comparison Technique

PAIRED COMPARISONS

	Management	Equipment	Memos	Writing	Mis-understanding	Jargon	Right person	Not listening	Red tape	Total	Ranking
Management	X	2	2	2	1	1	0	1	1	10	4
Equipment	0	X	1	1	0	0	0	0	1	3	8
Memos	0	1	X	2	1	1	0	0	1	6	6
Writing	0	1	0	X	0	0	0	0	1	2	9
Misunderstanding	1	2	1	2	X	1	1	1	2	11	3
Jargon	1	2	1	2	1	X	0	0	1	8	5
Right person	2	2	2	2	1	2	X	1	2	14	1
Not listening	1	2	2	2	1	2	1	X	2	13	2
Red tape	1	1	1	1	0	1	0	0	X	5	7

method also ensures through the discussion process a thorough understanding of the causes of the problems. The disadvantages of the method are that at times it can be difficult to justify why any particular problem is considered more important than another, there is a restriction on the number of comparisons that can be made (certainly any more than 15 make it very impractical unless computer facilities are available) and the method relies on a team's ability to come to a consensus which is not always easy to achieve.

Overall, however, it is an excellent way of demonstrating that some objective method has been used in establishing priorities and identifying the 'vital few' facts about a situation, particularly where no data is available. It is a method which can also be used in evaluating possible solutions in an objective way and trying to reach some consensus.

Once the vital few facts have been established about a particular quality problem, such as the major reasons for customer complaints or for poor communication within a department, it is necessary to analyze the probable causes of that problem in order to begin the process of moving towards likely solutions. One key method is to use cause and effect diagrams (sometimes called Ishikawa diagrams after Professor Ishikawa of Tokyo University). These are flow type diagrams based on defining the probable cause of a problem (identified through Pareto analysis or paired comparison) and then identifying the likely major variables or causes of that problem under the four M approach: materials, machines, manpower and methods. Figure 24 shows how the diagram can be

Figure 24 Cause and Effect Diagram: Faulty Orders

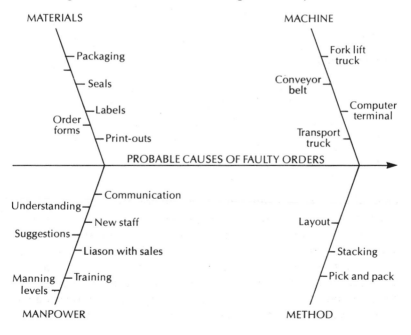

developed based on the probable causes of faulty orders within an organization. The four M approach has been developed on the basis that almost every situation within the work place is likely to be affected by the materials used to carry out a particular function, the machines used, however sophisticated or simple, the manpower involved in the work and the methods or processes which are used to carry out the particular function. In preparing the cause and effect diagram it is important to show on the diagram ALL probable causes of a problem even if some are rejected at a later stage in the analysis. This enables a problem solving group to get a clear picture of the particular situation which has been identified. In carrying out the detailed analysis it may become necessary to do two or more cause and effect diagrams, the initial one providing the overview of the situation and then, if one particular area plus its method or manpower is identified as a particular problem, a further detailed analysis based on that aspect. Once a cause and effect diagram has been completed it is necessary to identify the key causes of the problem which appear on the diagram and if necessary carry out a further paired comparison or collect data in order to establish more information.

If the cause and effect diagram is developed systematically and in detail, this provides a framework for a likely solution to a problem. For instance, the organization involved in looking at customer complaints was the mass male toiletries organization which had a large number of orders which were delivered faulty from a new computerized warehouse. An analysis of the probable causes of the problem indicated that by and large the new methodology linked to the machinery in use and the materials all worked fairly effectively and the biggest problem was in the manpower area. This pointed the way to the possible solutions which concentrated on better training and efforts to improve communication between the various departments and the warehouse. The process also ensured that all aspects of the probable causes were looked at in a comprehensive way. In this particular case, because the system was completely new, there was a suggestion that it was the equipment which was faulty or possibly the pick and pack method but, as indicated, the problem was centred on the people.

Another useful form of analysis is to use the matrix, which is a simple form either in a table or a chart of demonstrating a number of different variables at the same time. For instance, it can be used

Figure 25 Matrix of Errors by Assembly Operator

Error type	OPERATOR						Total
	A	B	C	D	E	F	
1	0	0	1	0	2	1	4
2	1	0	0	0	1	0	2
3	0	⑯	1	0	2	0	⑲
4	0	0	0	0	1	0	1
5	2	1	3	1	4	2	⑬
6	0	0	0	0	3	0	3
27							
28							
29							
Totals	6	⑳	8	3	㊱	7	80

to demonstrate the people, the error types and how many errors of each type are made by each person. An example of a matrix of errors is shown in Figure 25 which looks at individual performances against error types. The purpose of the matrix approach is to identify the interaction between the variables: for instance, to show that one individual may have a tendency to make certain errors – demonstrating possibly an individual training need – or it may show that an error type is common to all employees, which may indicate that there is a problem in the actual methodology.

Linked to this approach can be trend analysis which is designed to show whether time factors have a bearing on a particular problem. For instance, a particular key error type identified by the matrix could be analyzed by trend analysis if it is considered that a time analysis might reveal further features of the problem. An example of monthly errors by operators on an assembly line is set out in Figure 26. This would indicate that there are particular problems in particular months, which in turn may lead to analysis which would include looking at products produced during the month and any other features, either internal or external, such as absenteeism, inclement weather, holiday period and so on.

So far the techniques discussed have been relatively straightforward and simple and form the basis of much of the systematic problem solving that needs to be applied in a total quality programme, particularly through the task groups and the quality

Figure 26 Trend Analysis

Rank	Nov.	Monthly errors of assembly-line operators					Total
		Dec.	Jan.	Feb.	Mar.	Apr.	
1	4	1	0	0	0	0	5
2	1	2	0	5	1	0	9
3	3	1	0	3	0	3	10
4	1	1	0	2	2	4	10
5	0	1	0	10	2	1	14
6	2	1	0	2	2	15	22
7	2	4	1	11	1	7	26
8	2	0	0	7	23	7	39
9	6	3	0	18	9	4	40
10	13	4	0	10	10	9	46
11	15	8	2	11	10	3	49
12	6	6	5	18	6	10	51
13	7	2	1	28	25	1	64
14	16	8	1	14	11	15	65
15	2	16	8	22	8	23	79
16	22	18	1	33	7	13	94
17	18	8	3	37	9	23	98
18	16	17	0	22	36	11	102
19	27	13	4	62	4	14	124
20	6	5	2	61	22	29	125
21	39	10	2	45	20	14	130
22	26	17	4	75	31	35	188
Total	234	146	34	496	239	241	1390
% defective....	10.6	6.6	1.8	22.6	10.9	11.0	10.5

circles. As these groups become more sophisticated it may be necessary to introduce the concepts of statistical quality control (SQC) so favoured in Japan and considered the basis of much of their success in total quality. From experience I believe strongly that introducing the concepts of SQC too early in a total quality programme can create a lot of resistance, particularly if there is intensive teaching of statistics. Nevertheless it is important to introduce some of the basic concepts.

Two basic concepts underline SQC – product control, which in essence is the direct control of the product or service in terms of quality standards at each stage of a production or service cycle, by concentrating on achieving quality standards which eliminate defective material or service, and process control, which is the method by which quality is built into every stage of the process, enabling faults to be identified rapidly and then corrected.

Product control is centred on the decision at each stage of the customer/supplier network to accept or reject products. At one extreme, product control can operate through 100 per cent inspection which is both costly and is likely to be imperfect due to human error, or by sample inspections. As was indicated, in Canon Cameras in Japan this had been taken to a level where the whole system was based on sample testing. The key to success in product control is to design a sampling system which is consistent and provides management with information to monitor performance.

Process control is based on carrying out a series of measurements to establish the assignable causes for possible problems, to the point at which variations in performance are only as a result of random causes (see Chapter 9). The heart of the process is to establish a means of controlling the random variations and this can be done by the use of control charts.

The principle of using control charts is based on establishing a desired level of quality and then for random variations indicating the upper and lower levels of acceptability. As indicated in Figure 27, information is then collected to show performance over a period of time and also to indicate whether it is necessary to take corrective action or not. The principle behind statistical process

Figure 27 A Drift in Quality

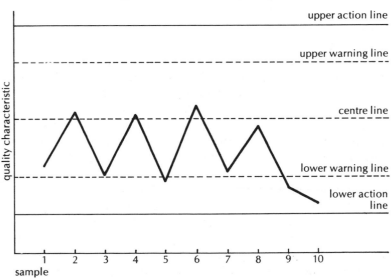

Source: K. A. Yeomans, *Statistics for the Social Scientist,*
Vol. 2: *Applied Statistics* (Penguin, 1968)

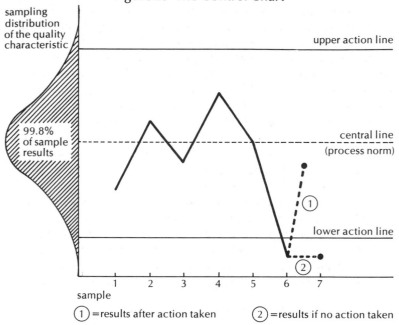

Figure 28 The Control Chart

① = results after action taken   ② = results if no action taken

Source: *Statistics for the Social Scientist,* Vol 2 (adapted)

control is the concept of normal distribution whereby in any given measuring situation it is likely that a very large number of samples will perform around the mean point of the distribution.

The techniques can be used to assess the degree of conformance to agreed specifications at all levels within the process, and can be used both within short runs and small batch manufacture as well as high volume manufacture. The use of statistical control is not only confined to manufacture and can be used for instance in large clerical offices to verify the accuracy of transactions being carried out as well as within other service industries to check methods of operation. As can be seen from Figure 28, the method provides a means of identifying when action needs to be taken in any particular situation.

Statistical quality control also has the advantage of providing a means of continually seeking improvements to processes by re-establishing standards at a higher level until gradually performance

standards become better and better. Within a total quality programme it is possible progressively to introduce more and more
sophisticated statistical techniques to assist in the programme, but
this is a long-term objective and as already emphasized it is essential that in the early stages the training does not involve a heavy
investment in the teaching of statistics.

Statistical quality control helps to improve performance by preventing the use of defective materials through product control and
ensuring that quality is maintained at the appropriate level through
process control. The main advantage is that it seeks out facts about
performance and creates an environment which is conducive to
effective problem solving.

The minimum requirements for introducing some form of SQC
within an organization are as follows:

- introducing the concept of normal distribution by showing
  that it occurs not only in sampling theory but in many natural
  phenomena. The IQs of children, the yield of a large number
  of plots planted with potatoes, the weights of people in the UK
  and the length of screws produced by a machine all have the
  characteristic bell-shaped distribution shown in Figure 29. In
  fact whenever a measurement is affected by a large number of
  small independent variables (random variations), none of
  which dominate, the distribution of the actual performance
  levels being measured will always have the characteristic of a

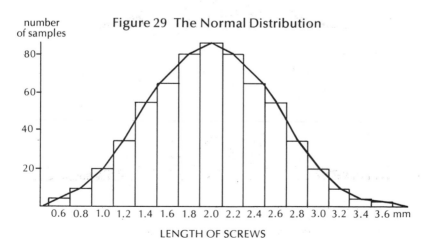

Figure 29 The Normal Distribution

number of samples

LENGTH OF SCREWS

Figure 30 Normal Distribution with Different Spreads

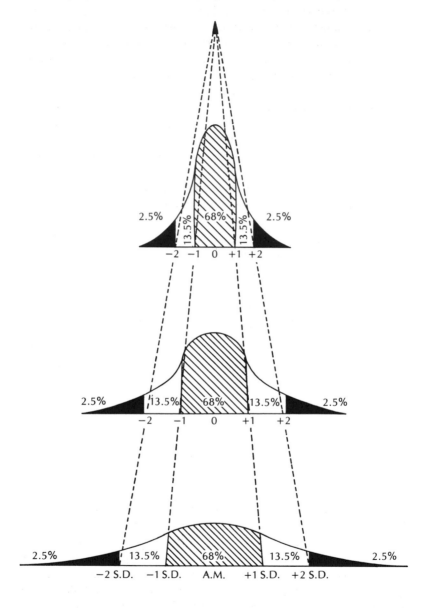

Source: *Statistics for the Social Scientist,* Vol. 2

normal distribution curve. It should be emphasized that normal distributions are not identical – some being broad with a wide range, others tall with a narrow range but they all share one key characteristic – the fact that measurement of standard deviation from the mean establishes the position beyond which known proportions of the total frequency lie. Figure 30 shows three normal distributions with standard deviations. Standard deviations are a method of measuring the amount of dispersion around an arithmetic mean, in other words the centre point of a normal distribution curve

● using control charts, which can be simply taught in terms of getting individuals to fill in – on a sample basis – performance levels on a form. This form shows performance against the established mean and allows for variations which are and are not acceptable. This in turn allows the employee to make the relevant adjustments to the performance levels. An example of the form is shown in Figure 31.

Figure 31 Control Chart Form

Sample	1	2	3	4	5	6	7	8	9	10
	2	0	2	1	2	3	−2	3	3	1
	−1	0	1	−1	2	−5	−2	2	−1	0
Results	−2	0	−1	−2	0	0	−1	−3	0	0
	1	1	−2	−3	0	−1	0	1	0	0
	0	1	0	3	0	−2	0	1	−1	−2

I have covered training on a modular basis outlining the key requirements as training in:

● concepts of quality
● interpersonal skills
● a variety of techniques.

Individual organizations must develop, often with some outside assistance at the outset, specifically tailored courses to meet the needs of their organization and its culture. The various training modules outlined in this chapter can be used flexibly to do this without disturbing the core elements of the modules. Specific examples/case studies based on the organization itself should be used to practise the various techniques. The essence of total quality training therefore is to build each module around practical work which individuals can relate back to. I would advocate that, in general, off the shelf or packaged training tends not to be so effective in a total quality programme.

Fundamentally the concept of continuous development needs to be extended to training. Total quality training should be occuring regularly for all levels, not just at the beginning of the programme. The training should seek to extend and develop understanding of the basic techniques.

In this way, as the Japanese have demonstrated and Crosby so forcefully put, you 'do it over again'.

Chapter 13
OPERATING ELEMENTS –
FACILITATOR TRAINING

One of the key roles for providing guidance and assistance to both task groups and in particular to quality circles within the overall programme is that of the facilitator. Particular responsibilities include:

- providing a link with senior management by reporting to the steering committee and to the total quality manager or equivalent giving reports on progress and ensuring that senior management continue to provide support to the total programme
- co-ordinating all the activities of the task groups and quality circles by ensuring that there is knowledge and understanding of all the different projects that have been undertaken to avoid overlap, repetition and possible conflict
- ensuring that the groups can get help from technical specialists either within or outside the organization. The facilitator helps to channel resources. This is a key responsibility in the sense that if circle/task group leaders spend time searching for specialist help and ensuring they attend meetings, this can cause problems and frustration. This arises because the specialists may be asked to meetings in a random way and the priorities are not always made clear to the specialists. By using the facilitator to access the specialists it is easy to be certain they provide the appropriate level of help
- ensuring management respond to proposals and presentations by keeping track of the proposals and checking that management's response is timely. One of the most demotivating aspects of quality circle activity can be that once a presentation is made management can take an inordinate time to respond in formal terms. This is partly because in the overall process the quality circle project is just one of many priorities

faced by management. In the eyes of circle members it is obviously a key priority, and the role of the facilitator is to ensure that management at least inform the circle/task group members of progress in implementation or decision making

● making practical arrangements for meetings. If only one hour a week is available to a group it is wasteful of time if there are practical problems getting into the meeting room

● liaising with the trade unions by setting up a regular dialogue to ensure the unions are aware of the total quality programme. At the same time the trade union representatives can raise problems or issues quickly and easily with the facilitator. This communication is better handled on an informal basis in the sense that it provides an opportunity for trade unions to raise issues or indeed fears or worries with the facilitator away from the normal channels of communication. At the same time it is appropriate on a more formal level for the facilitator to make presentations on progress to appropriate joint consultative bodies such as the works council. As I have already indicated the relationships with the trade unions are critical to the success of a total quality programme.

● monitoring the success of the programme, particularly in relation to quality circles, by providing reports and feedback on successful projects and ensuring a high level of publicity on the priniciple that success breeds success.

In order to help individuals carry out this overall role, facilitator training needs to concentrate on:

● ensuring the facilitator has a full understanding of all the methodologies used in the process – this is best carried out by ensuring that the facilitator attends both management training and task group/quality circle leader training courses. In the long run the facilitator would be responsible for running these courses

● providing a detailed outline of the functions which the facilitator needs to fulfil

● identifying some of the potential problems that may need to be resolved

● identifying some of the qualities required of a facilitator which in turn can lead to gradual awareness of some of the skills required.

In looking at the functions of a facilitator the role can be divided into two separate areas: assisting groups in the actual task of solving the problem, and providing help during the process. Assisting in the task involves:

- helping the group to identify potential projects – each time a group is due to start a new project it is important, particularly in the early stages of task groups/quality circles, to ensure that they take on a project which they are capable of resolving and which is not likely to take too long or be too complex
- advising the group and ensuring that the problem solving methodology is followed – groups which are not used to systematic problem solving have a tendency to lose their way. They often go straight to the answer stage without carrying out a proper analysis of the problem, which can undermine the whole methodology and lead to inappropriate solutions. At the same time the systematic approach can sometimes cause frustration in that it appears to the inexperienced pedantic and slow. Once a number of projects have been completed, the usefulness of the methodology becomes more apparent to the group
- helping in the use of the techniques which are often unfamiliar to the groups and require advice and guidance. This is particularly the case in some of the statistical techniques which, however well taught on a training course, may need reinforcement
- helping groups to decide on what action they will take in relation to implementing projects. This includes advice and guidance on whom to consult, whose commitment is needed, the best way to communicate changes and a timetable for implementation
- helping groups to recognize the possible outcomes of certain approaches – the facilitator should have a much wider view than individual departmental groups and may be able to advise groups that certain courses of action may not be appropriate or are being covered by other areas
- overcoming technical difficulties by giving or seeking advice on the more complex issues.

While assistance in the actual task of problem solving is a critical role for the facilitator, in many ways a more important role is helping the groups in the *process* of problem solving by:

- observing how the group is working and ensuring that all members are participating effectively with no interpersonal factors preventing effective group work
- counselling, especially the leader, but also group members about behaviour and leadership skills. Many of the leaders may be hugely inexperienced in running problem solving groups or in chairing meetings. Training courses in themselves are not sufficient to overcome these without further counselling or help
- motivating groups whose commitment and enthusiasm are bound to vary from time to time. I have found that after the initial enthusiasm, often related to the wide publicity associated with the launch of a programme, group members suddenly realize after about four or five weeks that problem solving is quite hard work
- achieving and keeping the commitment of middle management who are critical to the success of a total quality programme. The facilitator can achieve this by spending time talking to middle management about problems and issues, advising and counselling them on how they shoud respond when difficulties arise and at the same time reacting to practical problems raised by middle management, eg. where there is a conflict between production schedules and the need to release people for meetings. At the same time there is sometimes a tendency for middle management to allow the groups to operate without positively enquiring how they are progressing and the facilitator can help in bridging between middle management and the groups to ensure there is full understanding of what is going on
- ensuring communication at all levels by taking whatever action is necessary formally or informally to publicize the work of groups, particularly successes, and at the same time to avoid misunderstandings through poor communications.

In helping groups in the process of problem solving, a number of potential problems can arise which the facilitator needs to resolve, and in which he or she may need to provide counselling to the individuals concerned. These problems can include:

- domination by the leader – a common characteristic particularly in the early days of task groups or quality circles. This is primarily because the leader has usually already been on a training course and has some confidence while at the same time is anxious to ensure quick progress is made. Many inexperienced leaders do not appreciate how much they dominate discussions and try to impose their views on the group

● conflict between smaller sub-groups which make up the larger group. Within a group there may often be sub-groups where rivalries – for instance between two ends of a production line or between two sub-sections of a finance department – can cause conflict

● unequal participation, where two or three individuals completely dominate a group. Unless this is overcome individuals can become disillusioned and drop out of the group. At the same time biased views can begin to creep into group activity because of the domination of certain individuals. The facilitator can help draw out all group members and at the same time advise and counsel the leader how this can be achieved

● uneven use of group resources, whereby the detailed tasks are not properly allocated across the group or particular specialisms within the group are not properly used. I recall on one occasion within a task group involving a number of different departments that it was only towards the end of a problem solving activity that the group realized that an individual present was an expert in the field they were discussing. He was a quiet individual who did not push his views and in fact he himself became frustrated at times as he listened to the group talking nonsense

● overcoming a climate of defensiveness – at the beginning of any problem solving activity there is always a certain amount of concern and unease about exposing problems. This is particularly true when analysis of data has indicated that a great deal of the problem is based on, for instance, operator error, lack of training and general inability of the group members or their peers to complete the tasks properly. This can generate considerable defensiveness rather than be seen as a way of overcoming frustration. The facilitator again can play a role in helping groups overcome this and not worrying about the 'blame syndrome', whereby once problems are identified all that will happen is that people will be blamed for them. This is particularly so when management become involved, who may,

depending on the climate of the organization, have a tendency to become frustrated and angry rather than react positively
- providing creative alternatives to problems by helping groups to widen their perspective. The facilitator is in a unique position to take an objective view of a situation and encourage groups to more lateral thinking to seek creative long-term solutions to problems
- preventing restrictive communications – one of the key difficulties which can arise in quality circle activity is the tendency for the quality circle to set themselves up as a closed group, often regarded as elitist by their peers. This is not usually done deliberately but is a result of a certain amount of defensiveness on the part of the quality circle before they have achieved some firm results. This in turn creates suspicion from those outside the circle both among peers and management
- avoiding potential conflicts by spotting in advance where a solution may appear to fit a group but in fact could conflict with a wider approach being considered by management or indeed other groups.

In order to play a significant role both in helping groups in their tasks and in the process of problem solving, a facilitator needs to develop a number of skills. Some of these should perhaps already exist within the individuals who are chosen to act as facilitators. Nevertheless they can be developed. There is much debate on the appropriate training in this area for facilitators and I have found that provided there is a proper understanding of the function, already outlined, and a thorough knowledge of how the various techniques can be used, many of the softer skills are developed by counselling facilitators either by the external consultant, if used, or through the management training department. The skills which need development include:

- self awareness – in the sense that there is proper awareness of the impact the facilitator can have on individuals and groups
- awareness of others
- sensitivity to the group process – facilitators should have an awareness of the basics in group problem solving, but more important understand some of the underlying factors that help effective group working
- listening skills/ability to listen and use the ideas of others

- self confidence/assertiveness – provided these are carefully controlled
- communication skills – the ability to deal on a one-to-one basis with individuals at all levels and make regular presentations in a formal way
- objectivity – in one organization I attended two meetings within a morning. The first was where a facilitator was advising and counselling both the group leader and management to resolve a certain disagreement about the solution to a problem. After the meeting he privately told management that they needed to be more objective and less defensive. Later in the morning the facilitator found himself in the role of line manager where his own quality circle was making a presentation to him. Somewhat to my surprise I found that the facilitator had changed and had become much more subjective as his own department came under the scrutiny of a quality circle.

I have made reference to the need for a facilitator to have a degree of self-awareness and at the same time understand the behaviour and group processes involved in problem solving activity. While there are many models that can be used, one simple model has proved useful in helping facilitators understand a possible framework within which they can work.

This model is based on four behaviour styles:

- the expressive
- the driver
- the analytical
- the amiable.

While all individuals tend to combine all four behaviour styles, in many cases a single style will predominate. In being sensitive to individual and group situations, the facilitator needs to identify the most effective way of interacting with each style of behaviour.

Facilitator training is based on:

- ensuring a clear understanding of the role
- providing a behavioural framework to help the facilitator counsel others
- giving the facilitator confidence to play a key role in the total quality programme.

Chapter 14
OPERATING ELEMENTS – IMPLEMENTATION

Within the total quality process we now have an overall strategy which has been developed over some length of time, we have carried out detailed planning which includes a detailed timetable for implementation, management and the work force have been fully briefed and key individuals have been trained. We can now begin to move towards achieving results within the total quality framework. The implementation process involves the establishment of:

- a steering committee
- interdepartmental task forces
- improvement groups/quality circles.

Steering committee

In the overall process of implementing total quality, the activity of both task teams and improvement groups/quality circles needs to be managed. The framework within which they can be managed is the steering committee which is fundamental to the process and needs to be actively led by senior management. The steering committee therefore needs to be composed of either the managing director or a senior board member as previously indicated with responsibility for the total quality programme. Other members of the steering committee should include the total quality manager, the facilitator and key functional heads. It is possible to involve also a senior trade union official if appropriate. The role of the steering committee is to set priorities and allocate resources and ensure that projects meet their objectives. The senior management not only need to chair the steering committee, which should meet monthly, but in addition should play an active role in the whole programme.

Chairing the steering committee is not sufficient in itself to demonstrate commitment to the overall programme. The steering committee meets monthly (once the programme is fully under way), to review the detailed projects which have been completed and pull together the overall progress for the organization as a whole. It should be common practice for task groups and improvement groups/quality circles to report regularly on their progress to the steering committe and at least once a year there should be a major forum where all the leaders come together with the steering committee to review progress.

It is particularly important for task teams to produce action programmes for full approval by the steering committee, which identifies benefits measured through improved quality, improved customer service or cost reduction and indicates resource requirements and a timetable. Where conflicts arise between the action programme generated by different task teams, the steering committee should set the priorities. It is more difficult for a similar approach to apply to the improvement group/quality circle process, particularly at the beginning of the programme where there is likely to be some suspicion of an external group such as the steering committee. Once the programme is fully under way it is easy for the improvement groups to provide similar action programmes to the steering committee. As already indicated, the facilitator has a key role in advising both improvement groups/quality circles and the steering committee in order to avoid possible conflicts between the various groups.

Task groups

Task groups are multi-disciplinary teams set up by management aimed at solving specific problems. The composition of the teams and their objectives and choice of project are the specific responsibility of management. Typical projects tackled by task teams include organization or systems related projects such as reducing the amount of engineering time, which would involve production engineering and production planning, or improving the system for providing 'gift sets' samples to customers, which would involve marketing, design, sales and production. The teams are set up to work on a specific project or group of projects; once these have been completed successfully, they are disbanded and may be replaced by different teams with alternative projects or incorporated into the overall total quality programme. The main focus of the task teams is to achieve results as quickly as possible. Within this overall framework the actual methodology used by task teams is based on the systematic approach to joint problem solving and using many of the techniques covered under training in Chapter 12. The process of working on a single project, analyzing it in detail, coming up with solutions and presenting the solutions to management, including responsibility for implementation, are appropriate to the task group approach.

Some of the advantages involved in the task group approach are that:

● management can focus the efforts of the groups quite directly
● generally speaking quick results can be achieved
● they break down interdepartmental barriers
● they generate among middle management an understanding of the processes involved in a total quality programme and give them an opportunity to be directly involved
● they generate commitment to the programme.

While task groups can and do play a major role in a total quality programme, some care has to be exercised in managing their operation because there are certain disadvantages in the approach, such as that:

● with the agenda being set by management it can create problems and resentment because management's perception of the key issues may be different to the view of those involved in the task groups
● as they are often a group of peers between departments they are difficult to chair and require particular skills to manage the process
● if too many task groups are set up there is a danger that they generate a certain amount of frenetic activity which is difficult to control, particularly in overlapping solutions
● depending on the organizational climate and relationships between various departments they can focus some of the resentments and rivalries between departments, which, if not properly handled, can become explosive.

Since each task group is set up to work on one project it is likely that the individuals involved, other than the leaders, may not have been exposed to the problem solving activity involved although it is likely that some training has been carried out before for all task group members. In this environment it is important to ensure that as the project develops some basic disciplines are kept in managing the process and at the same time ensuring that people become familiar with the methodology. I have found that one useful way to do this is to ask the leaders to draw up a brief outline plan covering the likely agenda for the initial meetings and the likely total timetable for the project in hand. Before the task groups commence it is also important to establish the basic approach in terms of meeting times. In general task groups should meet weekly but probably for longer periods than one would anticipate for meetings of improvement groups or quality circles. Nevertheless there should be a discipline and the most effective approach is to allow for weekly meetings lasting no longer than two hours with provision for additional individual work to take place between each meeting, with each task group member being set particular tasks to carry out as appropriate. The time and dates of meetings should also be clearly established.

The likely agenda items for the meetings could include the following:

Meeting 1
- review total quality objectives
- focus on specific objectives/projects of group
- review basic methodology to be used in problem solving
- brainstorm possible causes of problem identified for first project
- agree likely timetable for overall project

Meeting 2
- identify how analysis of current conditions should take place and in particular how facts about the current situation should be collected
- allocate tasks within group to set about collection of data
- identify period of data collection or, if historical records are to be used, length of time that needs to be taken into account in researching historical records

Meetings 3–8
- analyze data collected
- analyze likely causes of problems
- develop solutions

Meetings 9–10
- prepare presentation to management
- practice presentation.

Clearly the number of meetings required to resolve a particular problem or work on a project may be greater or less depending on the nature of the project. Nevertheless this broad outline gives an indication of the typical length of time that a task group may take to complete a project.

Improvement groups/quality circles

Throughout this book I have tended to refer to 'improvement groups' and 'quality circles' interchangeably. In implementing any particular programme the first thing that needs to be decided, probably by management, is which approach or wording should be used. While not an essential feature in itself, it nevertheless can send messages to the organization as a whole in terms of how the total quality programme is to be managed. 'Quality circles' is the traditional name and I have found that in general that term is most appropriate within manufacturing industry and tends not to carry a jargon tag, which can be the reaction to it outside manufacturing. It emphasizes the message of quality in an appropriate way. In many sevice organizations the term 'improvement groups' is more common, partly because management wish to create an environment of improvement in all aspects of the services provided. Other titles can include 'customer care groups', 'quality of service groups', 'service improvement groups'. There is no right answer but management do need to decide what the most appropriate title is within their organization. For the purposes of this section I will refer to the groups as improvement groups.

As has already been indicated in Chapter 11, improvement groups are quite different to task groups in that they are confined to people working within the same work area, usually composed of those at the operational or front line end of the work. They are voluntary, can choose their own projects and are often led by the first line supervision or junior management. They meet generally for one hour a week.

The introduction of improvement groups into an organization is an essential ingredient of the total quality programme because without improvement groups it is not possible to involve directly the shop floor or office workers in the total quality programme. If one accepts in particular that a total quality programme should be based on a participative management approach, it is even more important to ensure there is direct shop floor involvement in the process. It also provides an opportunity for training in quality techniques to be extended to all levels within the organization. Having said this, the actual process of introducing improvement groups within the organization needs to be carried out in a more controlled approach than that for task groups. There is a need to seek volunteers and win the commitment and interest of the shop floor in the whole process as well as the specific involvement with the improvement groups.

As a result the approach to improvement groups is significantly different to that adopted for task groups. At this stage in the process there has been extensive briefing and there is an understanding of what is involved. Additionally, following the briefing process the improvement group leaders should have been identified, training been carried out and volunteers been sought from the shop floor or the office to form the groups.

Against this background there are a number of prerequisites which apply in the successful introduction and operation of improvement groups, as follows:

● there should be a modest, quiet introduction of the groups by starting on a pilot basis, probably involving between six and eight groups initially depending on the size of the organization. This allows the process to be tested to show results can actually be achieved and to win the confidence of both middle management and the shop floor. In determining the number of improvement groups that should be used in the pilot, attempts should be made to involve a cross-section of the operations including, in manufacturing industry, office operations. The number of groups should be sufficient to ensure that the random failure of one or two groups for reasons outside anybody's control does not influence the whole programme.

- there should be an understanding at all levels that the board and senior management are committed not just to the total quality programme, which is obviously essential, but to the specific operation of improvement groups. In particular they should be physically seen to be taking an interest in the operation of the groups and at appropriate times should review with groups their achievements
- middle management and supervision need to be involved in the process and be consulted about the best way to introduce groups within their area of responsibility. As I have already indicated (see Chapter 8), it is useful to involve middle management in actually designing the implementation programme as part of their own training in the total quality programme. This tends to win their commitment and interest for the whole process. Additionally, the improvement group process does involve delegation of decision making to the lowest practicable level so that proposals being put forward by the groups can be agreed and implemented as quickly as possible. In Japan considerable success has been achieved in delegating this authority primarily to supervisory level, with middle management being involved in wider co-ordinating issues. The practicality of doing this depends on the organization and the operations involved but the principle of delegated decision making is essential to the success of improvement groups
- training of improvement group leaders is critical to the success of the groups. In addition it is important to provide some training to group members within the framework of the meetings. After the initial projects have been carried out I have also found it useful to carry out short top-up training (no more than two hours) for group members to extend their knowledge particularly in some of the statistical techniques. Provision also needs to be made for the training of new group members who can often be very disruptive to groups if they do not understand the processes
- the appointment of a facilitator to assist the improvement groups and provide help and guidance is also essential and in general there is considerable evidence to suggest that no improvement group activity has survived for long within organizations without such an appointment
- the support and understanding should be sought of trade

unions in a unionized environment by briefing the trade union representative. In this respect it is sometimes useful to produce guidelines and assurances regarding the work of improvement groups, emphasizing in particular that they do not have responsibility for covering pay and conditions, which is clearly the responsibility of the trade unions in unionized environments

● measurement of results on an ongoing basis and publicity as improvement groups succeed is important to provide a basis for the extension of improvement groups after the pilot phase. At the same time this ensures there is a clear message to all concerned that all levels are participating in the total quality programme. Most organizations who have company newspapers will usually use such media to publicize the work of improvement groups carrying appropriate pictures of both their successes and the groups themselves. This has a major impact on the morale and motivation of individual groups and extends knowledge across the organization as a whole.

The groups are now ready to meet but a few important decisions remain particularly in relation to the timing and location of each meeting. The responsibility for organizing this involves both the group leader and the facilitator, probably in discussion with the local management or departmental head. If the right time has not been chosen in relation to the work environment and the pressures on work or production, this will eventually cause the groups considerable difficulties.

Generally in manufacturing and on production lines the organization of group meetings is comparatively easy because, once agreed with the departmental manager, cover can be provided or the meetings can be arranged for times when the line is shut down during the week for maintenance.

Within office environments, while difficult to generalize, I have found that the best time is usually the hour either immediately before or immediately after the lunch period. Whatever the final decision, it needs careful evaluation and monitoring on an on-going basis in case there is a need to change because disruption is occuring. Within the service sector the establishment of a time for the improvement group requires a careful evaluation of client needs. Another aspect of establishing the timing is the actual frequency of meetings. As a general rule they should be held on a weekly basis although some flexibility is required either where it is inappropriate, such as for sales representatives, or where a shift cycle is being worked. The timing and frequency of meetings are part of the discussions and agreement with management. Once these are agreed it is important that they are strictly adhered to.

One final aspect about the timing and frequency of meetings is the cycle of meetings during the year. Many improvement groups who operate in environments where there are staggered holidays try to struggle through during the peak holiday period of July, August and early September, usually with one or two members always missing. This tends to be very disruptive to the groups and a great deal of repetitive work is done as those who have been on holiday either challenge what has been done or need to be brought up to date with events while they were away. As a result it is far better when a project is completed near to the main holiday period that the group makes a conscious decision to suspend group operations for this period and sets a specific date for the next meeting and the beginning of a new project. It is also useful if at all possible to have agreement on the likely next project before the group is suspended for the holiday period.

The location of the improvement group meetings and the facilities provided are important to the success of the groups. On large manufacturing sites difficulties can occur because often there are not many meeting rooms available which are easily accessible to a particular group. Additionally there is often competition for limited meeting room space. The basic approach should be that a group should meet in the same meeting room each week.

The most novel approach was within the major seafoods organization which used a portacabin as its improvement group meeting room. The cabin was fitted out for meeting room purposes and at the same time used for training generally. It represented the visible top management support of the total quality programme as well as of the improvement groups themselves. Clearly this may be regarded as an expensive solution but in relation to the total quality programme the cost was relatively small. The other advantage was that it was positioned in such a way that it was easily accessible both to the office staff and the production staff involved in the process.

Finally the facilities within the room are important. The lack of practical equipment is often regarded as a symbol of mangement's lukewarm attitude to the programme as a whole or at least to the improvement groups themselves.

The practical arrangements are a key aspect of the success of improvement groups and are often overlooked in the drive to establish a total quality programme within an organization. Nevertheless as a checklist the following points must be covered:

- timing
- frequency
- location
- facilities.

The likely agenda items for improvement group meetings follow to some extent the pattern of the task group but the pace is often slower because it is useful at the beginning of each meeting in the early stages to use up to about 10 to 15 minutes for the training of members in the various techniques. Improvement group members in general find it much easier to learn each technique as it arises and becomes useful, rather than cover all the techniques at the beginning, some of which may not come up for some considerable time. The biggest danger of this approach however is that they sometimes do not see the whole of the problem solving activity and become frustrated that they do not appear to be achieving results. At the beginning of the process therefore it is often useful to cover the overall problem solving activity in broad terms and if at all possible use some sort of visual aid to explain the process. There are a number of videos or tape slide presentations which explain the process in a straightforward way. In addition a considerable number of the organizations with which I have been involved have produced short videos showing the problem solving cycle by taking an example of an actual group. If neither approach is feasible then the material produced at the leader training course, which provides an indication of the problem solving activity using real problems and examples, can be presented by the leaders to provide an overview of the activity. The possible agenda for the initial meetings of improvement groups could include the following:

Meeting 1
- leader to report back on leader training course and explain some broad principles, possibly showing a video presentation
- review the role of the group members and general codes of conduct (ie highly participative)

- introduce concept of brainstorming perhaps using a 'fun' example
- confirm meeting time is appropriate
- review programme objectives
- initial brainstorm on possible first project

Meeting 2
- further brainstorm of possible initial projects
- refinement of brainstorm list
- introduce concept of paired comparisons as a method of establishing priority for first project
- agree on first project

Meeting 3
- initial brainstorm on likely causes of first problem
- review the problem solving process
- agree broad timetable for problem solving activity and main activities necessary to achieve a result
- identify how data is collected on current conditions, if necessary producing a data collection form

Meeting 4
- review initial data collection methodology and if necessary make amendments
- identify period of data collection and length of time necessary to achieve meaningful results
- check on definition of problem and redefine as appropriate
- check on project completion timetable and make necessary amendments

Meetings 5-10
- analyze data collected, introducing concept of Pareto analysis as appropriate
- analyze likely causes of problems, introducing concept of cause and effect diagrams as appropriate
- develop solutions

Meetings 11-14
- develop solutions and check with peer group outside the improvement group on acceptability of solution, if necessary organizing presentation during improvement group meeting
- develop implementation action plan
- prepare presentation to management
- practise presentation.

As with the task groups the number of meetings actually required to resolve a problem will vary depending on the nature of the project. For the early projects it is probably best to try to aim for a completion date in under 10 weeks from the beginning. Bearing in mind the cycle of problem solving which is required, this means that the leader, supported as appropriate by the facilitator, really does have to drive through the first project. It also emphasizes how important it is that the first project is a comparatively easy one and that an early result can be achieved which is likely to be acceptable to management. Quite often I have found it useful to encourage a group to do as a first project something where the solution is almost self-evident but requires the systematic problem solving approach. This also provides the opportunity to introduce the various techniques. For instance at one big chemical works the electricians identified as one of their biggest and most aggravating problems the fact that they did not each have an isolation key to isolate plant and equipment when they were working on it. The key was held in the foreman's office and apparently this system had been introduced some years previously by a now retired senior engineer. The solution to the problem was clearly going to be that each electrician should have an isolation key for which they were responsible. Nevertheless it was possible to introduce the concepts of problem solving by carrying out an analysis of the amount of time the electricians wasted travelling to and from the foreman's office to collect the key. Often the key was not available because someone else had it anyway. They were able to cost the solution and of course prepare a detailed presentation to management showing how expensive the current system was in terms of time and lost production. The whole problem solving activity took some five/six weeks to complete but had the advantage of introducing the techniques to the electricians in the group, achieving a quick result and demonstrating to management the possible savings that could be generated from even the simplest projects.

With the completion of each project the groups become more confident and of course more sophisticated, and are able to work through the systematic problem solving approach at a faster pace, introducing new and more sophisticated techniques as they go along. Once the initial learning has been completed, one can expect groups to produce between four to six projects per annum although there is some evidence to suggest that the longer the groups are in operation, the smaller the number of projects being completed in any one year, as they move on to wider and more difficult problems which take longer to resolve. Certainly the measure of success should not be based entirely on the number of problems being successfully solved during, for instance, a one year period. Broader measurements such as savings achieved or improvements in processes and general quality standards are required. The Japanese, for instance, place much greater emphasis on ensuring that people are continuously involved in problem solving activity to the extent that the end result for any one group is not measured just by the number of successful projects. The reason for this is because the principle of continuous improvement is achieved in practice by involving people long term in the problem solving activity. Some western analysts have concluded from this that much of the activity in improvement groups in Japan is largely wasteful of time. This misinterprets the position entirely, for the issue is much more about achieving long-term commitment and changes of attitude, which are more difficult to measure.

The presentation

The presentation of a project to management is a key step in the whole problem solving activity. It demonstrates to management that the group has thoroughly researched the project and has come up with a solution which is viable and cost effective. Particularly the first presentation of a group but even the first few are important in demonstrating to management just how effective and professional the group is and how much they have developed. The impact of these early presentations can change the climate within an organization quite dramatically as management begin to recognize the extent of the knowledge, experience and talent within their work force. Preparation for the presentation is therefore critical to give each member confidence and make sure the presentation hangs together properly.

One of the enduring debates about the improvement group process is the extent to which the presentation should be done by the leader, who after attending the leader training course has had some experience and direct training, or whether it should include each member of the group. The theory on effective presentations will tell you that the best presentation should be done by a single person, probably the leader, who is effective, well-trained and able to create an impact. While this may be ideal theory, I am convinced that within the improvement group process the concept of involving each member in the presentation creates a major impact, generates the commitment of all group members and can be most effective. Organizing such a presentation with a balanced structure is important and one has to appreciate that individual members who have often had no experience of any sort of public speaking at all are initially extremely nervous. This however can add to the impact as management recognize that despite the nervousness an excellent presentation is made. Interestingly enough, from experience of many presentations I have found that the more senior the group, the less effective the presentation and the smaller the impact of the visual aids. Some of the creativity used in visual aids has at times been quite outstanding.

In order to help the groups structure their presentation, the following approach can sometimes be useful:

(a) the leader introduces the presentation by:

● brief history of the group (if appropriate) and when project was started
● definition of project and brief summary of basic points
● introduction of each group member and reference to the part of the presentation that each will address
● request that questions are kept to the end of the presentation (this is important in a multi-person presentation where questions can be quite disruptive to the flow of the presentation)

(b) first group member provides definition of problem by:

● describing the brainstorming of the list of problems and how it was decided to select the project being carried out
● detailed definition of the problem and reasons why it was important to resolve it – such as the effect of problem on costs, customer service or lost time

(c) second member describes initial analysis of the causes of the problem showing:

● the cause and effect diagram
● the analysis of the most likely causes of the problem

(d) third member shows how following the intial analysis the group gathered data on the problem:

● describing the data collection procedures used such as a survey, questionnaire or checklist
● showing an analysis of the data using Pareto analysis or any other charts or graphs which have been prepared to demonstrate the issues involved

(e) the fourth member should be responsible for confirming the major causes of the problem described in the analysis of the data and setting out:

● possible solutions
● the criteria against which solutions were measured and how the particular solution being put forward was chosen
● describing in detail the solution being put forward

(f) the fifth member should be responsible for the selling in of the idea to management by:

● outlining the advantages of the solution
● providing a cost benefit analysis

(g) the sixth member should outline the plan of action by:

● describing how the solution is to be implemented
● indicating the expected implementation date
● describing the expected results
● describing how the group will evaluate the solution and follow up on the results

(h) the leader should be responsible for the final summary and the specific request to management for agreement to the proposal.

The impact of a presentation can be affected by the quality and appropriateness of the visual aids, which should highlight and illustrate the key points of the presentation. The first thing the group has to decide is the most appropriate form of visual aid for their presentation – flipchart, written report or viewgraph. It may be of course that a combination of these approaches is used to gain maximum impact but it should be kept clear, simple and relevant. Depending on the complexity of the problem the group should aim to spend some 30 minutes on their formal presentation, allowing a further 30 minutes for discussion with management. Presentations should generally take place during the normal improvement group meeting times even if this involves management attending on the night shift. It demonstrates management's commitment and at the same time keeps to the cycle of meetings and to the discipline of the one-hour meeting.

The groups should, in consultation with the facilitator, be certain that all interested parties from management attend the meeting and in particular that the decision makers are present. Normally one would expect the departmental head, who in most cases should be the decision maker, to attend the meeting supported by other managers and also functional management from other areas who have a direct interest or likely comment on the proposals being put forward by the group.

Management's response to the group should always be clear and positive. I have attended a considerable number of presentations where a defensive management have reacted in a hostile and negative way. The facilitator plays a key role in briefing management ahead of a meeting, not on any details of the presentation but how they should respond. Sometimes management feel as though they need to make an instant decision which is often wholly inappropriate. I can recall a number of occasions in early presentations where a senior manager or director was present with the departmental manager and felt it necessary to agree instantly to the proposals. When departmental management subsequently analyzed the solution they did not agree in full with the proposals. This caused not a little frustration within the group, who thought their project had been agreed.

On balance management should always give a measured response indicating how long they need to analyze the proposals put forward and the likely date for their reply. Whatever happens it is important that at the end of the meeting, management clearly summarize what action is going to be taken so that there is no misunderstanding about what has been agreed, what requires further discussion and the likely implementation date (if appropriate).

Reasons for failure

The key aspects of improvement group and task group activity have now been described, illustrating the typical cycle which occurs within the meetings and indicating the approach to presentations. If the structured approach outlined is followed, many of the obvious pitfalls that occur during task/improvement group activity will be prevented. Nevertheless there are some major factors which can influence the success of improvement group activity. Dr Barrie Dale from UMIST, one of the few academics to conduct research into improvement groups, has shown that there are a number of factors which can play a significant role in determining the success of improvement groups within organizations. He researched companies who were using improvement groups both in the manufacturing sector but also in the service sector. In considering the research results one of the issues which comes to light is: what is meant exactly by improvement group failure? For instance, if an improvement group has been operating for a number of years and then ceases to operate, is this a failure or simply a decision to suspend operations as a group decides that it has completed a successful series of projects and now wishes to take a break? On balance this is probably not a failure.

Nevertheless the results would indicate some important lessons can be learnt from the UMIST research. Some of the conclusions of the research were contained in an article in *Personnel Management* in February 1985 which Barrie Dale and I wrote looking at 'Quality circles – why they break down and why they hold up'. In the article, drawing on the research, 20 major reasons for quality circle failure were identified. Figure 32 sets out the results of the research.

As can be seen, the majority of the first 10 problems could be regarded as management related problems or those outside the control of the circle itself, such as labour turnover. However, this emphasizes firstly the importance of ensuring complete commitment particularly of middle management and first line supervision, and secondly the proper briefing of everybody involved. Looking at the specific operation of groups it is also interesting to note that some of the major reasons for failure included delays in responding to the recommendations, and over-ambitious projects tackled – both of which can be overcome by proper organization and

Figure 32 Reasons for Quality Circle Failure

	Reasons for failure *(Companies were asked to identify no more than four main reasons for each circle failure)*	Number of quality circles failing (N=249)	Number of companies quoting that reason (N=42)
1	Redundancies and/or company restructuring caused by economic situation	54	18
2	Labour turnover (transfers, promotions, etc)	48	17
3	Circle leaders lacked time to organize meetings	45	16
4	Lack of cooperation from middle management	45	13
5	Lack of cooperation from first-line supervisors	34	9
6	Circle members disillusioned with quality circle philosophy	30	12
7	Circles ran out of projects to tackle	27	13
8	Delay in responding to circle recommendations	20	7
9	Leader not following through initial training	19	1
10	Over-ambitious projects tackled	18	8
11	Lack of management recognition of contribution	18	5
12	Circle members lacked time to carry out activities	17	10
13	Groups spread over too wide a work area	10	9
14	Management change – new manager not picking up leader responsibilities	10	1
15	Failure to get solutions implemented	9	5
16	Inadequate training	8	4
17	Lack of support from facilitator	8	3
18	Lack of extrinsic rewards/motivation	6	3
19	Trade unions withdrew support due to dispute	5	2
20	Ideas pre-empted by non-circle members	5	2

Source: *Personnel Management*, February 1985

communication with the support of the facilitator. As we commented in the article, 'the failure of 249 circles was reported and 39 different causes were cited which suggests that the pitfalls encountered in operating circles were many and varied and there is certainly no easy cookbook recipe to prevent failure'.

Also interesting are the results of the survey which show in Figures 33 and 34 the most common reasons for blue- and white-collar circle failures.

The results on blue-collar circle failure would indicate that the main reasons are strategic, in the sense that they tend to involve scepticism, fear, and management and trade union issues. On the other hand the results on the white-collar side indicate a much more

Figure 33 Why Blue-collar Circles Failed

Scepticism	
Fear of job losses	
Threat to trade union representation	
Management claim savings	
Challenge trade union practices	
Undermine shop steward	
Other	

%   10   20   30   40

Source: *Personnel Management,* February 1985

Figure 34 Why White-collar Circles Failed

Immediate supervisor's attitude	
Lack of projects	
Staff movement	
Leader's lack of time	
Redundancies/economic situation/disillusionment	

%   10   20   30   40   50   60

Source: *Personnel Management,* February 1985

locally based set of reasons for quality circle failure. As has been consistently indicated throughout the book, the strategic reasons for failure can be tackled by a proper approach to the whole project using the S-P-O approach. The results on the white-collar failures which support my own experience show that many of the problems are centred on the immediate area. Often – although this is a terrible generalization – white-collar supervisors/section leaders tend to be appointed for their technical ability rather than their management skills. This will increase the likelihood of concern and fear among such individuals about more participative management. The second issue highlighted in the results is the lack of time, which is often a problem in pressurized white-collar areas. There is also the problem of defining projects which arises from the fact that within white-collar areas there are often many small sub-groups who do not necessarily have common interests. As a result they find it difficult to define projects which affect the whole group. The companies in the manufacturing survey claimed that on average for every £1 spent on quality circles they received a return of £3.60 while in the service sector the average benefit/cost ratio was 2.4:1. The survey also found that successful introduction is dependent on a number of prerequisites. These included senior management commitment, support and recognition – in particular that of the chief executive – a properly planned and structured introduction, the appointment of a good facilitator, a high level of support for quality circles in the organization and effective and well trained leadership.

Despite some apparent negative findings from the research carried out by Barrie Dale, the conclusions we drew from the article still remain true today.

First and most important is that quality circles can be introduced successfully in the UK manufacturing and service sector environments, bringing measurable benefits to organizations and employees alike.

Chapter 15
MAKING IT HAPPEN

'No lasting achievement is possible without a vision and no dream can become real without action and responsibility' RM Kanter (When Giants Learn to Dance).

This sums up the approach advocated in this book about how to set about the implementation of a total quality programme. Yet there is a great deal of evidence to suggest that many total quality programmes are failing to sustain momentum and to achieve the results hoped for. In fact, disappointed with the results of their quality programmes, some organizations have begun to think that quality improvement is nothing more than yet another fad which is expensive to implement with little return on the investment. Many organizations, it would seem, still think that quality is just a quick fix. They do not seem to have accepted one of the basic issues behind quality management: that customer satisfaction can be directly linked to quality of customer service and that this can lead to increased revenue.

Tom Peters predicted in the eighties that the vast majority of total quality programmes would probably fail, indicating that one of the main reasons for this would be the lack of top management commitment.[1] More recently, an IPM report on total quality has produced some interesting results.[2] These showed that 83% of organizations surveyed experienced problems in implementation for two main reasons:

- resistance to change in the organizational structure
- resistance of middle management.

In addition, the long-term nature of total quality was demonstrated by other results of the survey: 22% of firms indicated that they had been successful after five years, whereas only 7% indicated that they had been successful where they had been operating a total quality programme for less than two years. All the evidence suggests that organizations find the transformation required in any total quality programme extremely difficult. The approach advocated in this book of *strategy, planning and operations* (S-P-O) can only provide a framework, but does not guarantee success.

Total quality demands fundamental changes in how an organization is managed and structured, how processes are set up and run, and how people contribute and behave. These changes cannot be achieved overnight, and the long-term nature of the process has the potential for creating conflict and tension in many western-run organizations, where the pressure is almost always on short-term results. Total quality is about the long-term success of an organization and about investment for the future, as argued so cogently by Deming so many years ago. The fundamental problems for any organization, therefore, are:

● to sustain the momentum
● to keep the vision
● to achieve some short-term results which generate further momentum for change.

If so many organizations are failing to achieve success through their total quality programmes, even if their approach to implementation follows the S-P-O approach, there is a need to understand better the reasons for this failure to maintain momentum and achieve the desired results.

Before considering possible reasons for failure in more detail, it is important to dispel a number of myths which are often associated with major change programmes:

● rapid results can be achieved ('quick fix')
● resistance is inherently wrong ('dump the doubters')
● all plans must be perfect before implementation ('fine tune forever')
● people don't really change ('old dogs can't learn new tricks')

These are considered in more detail below.

Rapid results can be achieved

There is often confusion between the need to achieve short-term results in the implementation of a total quality programme and the long-term nature of the approach. As I have already indicated, the Japanese in particular have demonstrated the importance of the long-term nature of continuous improvement and the never-ending search for quality. However, when organizations consider the implementation of total quality, they must recognize that short-term results can be achieved and, certainly in their planning and operations, they must gear themselves up to achieve some short-term results in order to satisfy business needs. Nevertheless, the real benefits, as argued by Deming, come from long-term investment and from long-term change in the attitudes of everyone within the organization. Top management often become frustrated because they are unable to demonstrate in the short term that attitudes, and therefore culture, have begun to change. But it is important that top management recognize, as they embark on a total quality programme, that the culture change inherent in total quality is a long-term process.

Resistance is inherently wrong

Commitment to change can only be achieved once individuals and groups within organizations have been brought into the change process. In order to do so, it is important that individuals within organizations feel free to challenge the relevance of total quality within the organizational framework and as regards business needs as well as to question the more detailed aspects of implementation. Top management will often confuse a healthy scepticism with outright resistance.. People have to go through the 'pain barrier' of change if they are to recognize the benefits of a fundamentally different approach to managing the organization. The major tenets of total quality are underpinned by the concept of continuous improvement, which, by definition, means that people must be allowed to look for different ways of doing things and of improving the approach – including the overall strategy for implementing total quality. A questioning workforce is likely to be a much more committed workforce if they feel their views are taken into account. Clearly, it would be naive to suggest that all resistance is merely challenge and questioning; there are always circumstances where resistance indeed stems from a determination not to change and to undermine the programme for whatever reason. But it has to be accepted that people do not like fundamental change and they will only embrace it if they are allowed to participate in its development and question and challenge the need for it.

All plans must be perfect before implementation

However well the S-P-O approach has been developed, it is inevitable that, particularly at the strategy and planning stages, not every circumstance will have been foreseen, not every plan will be perfect. One sure way to deflect the implementation of a change programme such as total quality is to eternally fine-tune the approach at the strategy and planning stage on the grounds that the proposed strategy or plans are not perfect and 'will not work'. Total quality implies testing, experimentation and, as often mentioned, continuous improvement. The first plans are unlikely to be perfect, or may not even be the right plans, but at least they have the benefit of providing a framework within the overall vision set out in the strategy. Markets will change, business and economic environments will change, and the total quality programme will need to be adjusted in detail to reflect these changes, particularly the business priorities at any given time. Plans by their very nature will never be perfect, so the aim has simply to be to ensure that the strategy is clear and that initial plans have been developed so that the programme can commence. Any plans will need to be adjusted in the light of experience and events. Do not wait until there is the 'perfect solution' or the programme will never start.

People don't really change

This particular view stems from concerns that, while people may at least in the short term change behaviour, they are unlikely to change attitudes and, therefore, when a programme loses momentum they will quickly revert to type. The problem comes from misunderstandings about attitudes, and ultimately culture change, within an organization. People will not change attitudes simply because they are told to do so, any more than organizations will change culture simply because the chief executive decides that a new culture needs to apply within the organization.

The classic example of this arose within Ciba-Geigy with the shop steward 'George' referred to in previous pages. George was a traditional shop steward within a chemical works and had many of the attitudes towards management and change associated with the more traditional shop stewards. Nevertheless, he was interested in the total quality programme, if only to defend his members' rights. We involved him directly in the training, taking him away to the management training centre. We sought his views on how we could structure the approach within his particular area and we gave him some of the tools and techniques necessary to begin the process of continuous improvement. We did not challenge, although often debated, his attitudes. We simply began the process of implementing total quality, demonstrating by results the benefits to him, his members and the organization. Over a period of time, as results were achieved, his attitudes began to change. I remember him on one occasion debriefing his team (and union members) following attendance at a three-day training event at the management training centre. He started off by saying that he fully expected three days of propaganda and was somewhat surprised to find that the approach was quite different. His behaviour and his actions began to change and to influence not only his attitudes but also those of his immediate team. Thus, in time, one began to see the change in culture expected within a total quality programme. The issue was that people do not change because we tell them to do so. They change because they learn from their experience that a particular change is worthwhile and brings benefits to them and those around them.

The reasons for failure

It is necessary to dispel the myths outlined above when implementing a total quality programme, but this is clearly not enough. As indicated, the evidence suggests that there continue to be problems with the implementation of total quality programmes, even if on the surface organizations follow the well-tried routes of implementation as outlined in the S-P-O approach. We need to understand better, therefore, from the experience of over 10 years of total quality implementation within the UK, what it is that is causing these problems. The evidence would suggest that there are probably three categories of reasons that underlie some of the problems:

- how a total quality programme is actually implemented
- the existing culture and structure of the organization
- management attitudes and actions.

These are considered in more detail below.

Approach to implementation

The main cause of the problems associated with the implementation of total quality is that senior management in organizations often fail to realize that they have embarked on a fundamental change of how the organization is managed and run. In order to compete, organizations are seeking to improve their business performance by changing organizational structures and work practices. Management layers are being cut out to save costs and to bring decision-makers closer to the action and to responsibility for product or service quality. A key part of a total quality programme is that responsibility should be diffused throughout the organization. This sort of change is about attitudes and you cannot ordain changes in attitudes.

The allure of total quality is such that it disguises the difficulties that organizations face in trying to introduce it. The message is 'upbeat' and 'can do', but it does not take account of the problems which organizations face in managing an organization-wide change that is at once ideal but extremely difficult to achieve at shop-floor and office level. Expectations are raised but often people are not provided with any means of doing things differently to meet these expectations. They walk around wondering what they can do today that was better from yesterday. People use the jargon of total quality and are seduced by the buzz words of 'empowerment' and 'culture change', but the capability of the organization does not always live up to the language. It is still using the old and often useless systems and methods. For instance, the computer or financial systems may remain unchanged, thereby hindering progress on the total quality programme.

The key issue is, therefore, that failure often occurs when

organizations seek large-scale change without first understanding the very thing they want to change – their own organization. What happens is that many organizations try to do too much at once instead of focusing early quality efforts on a few well-defined areas. The approach is often too amorphous and on too wide a scale, and the process of implementation is too long and without any defined milestones. The problem seems to be that those driving the implementation of total quality have taken on board the breadth and depth of the necessary change, but want to achieve this too quickly without recognizing that much of the change will take time. They do not appreciate that 'time' in this instance is measured in years, rather than months.

Within this overall framework there are a number of specific issues which seem to cause difficulties in implementation:

● There is often not enough analysis of the external and internal issues facing the organization or this is done too superficially. The people within the organization, therefore, have an insufficient understanding of customer requirements or the internal processes which apply. The initial analysis in developing the strategy is clearly important, but similar analysis needs to be carried out on a regular basis within the cycle of continuous improvement. It is not enough to do it just once. To some extent this problem arises from the fact that in a number of organizations there is a failure to place total quality at the heart of the business processes. It is not just a question of integrating quality into business strategy – quality must be at the core of business strategy.

● There is often a lack of problem measurement as a basis for quality improvement and, as a result, organizations fail to establish their quality priorities. It is essential that organizations quantify the potential market damage of various customer problems and focus the attention of their total quality programme on the most serious problems. In addition, organizations have not made an effort to quantify the market pay-off of improving quality. There is a tendency to view quality as different from any other regular business activity because it is often considered intangible, despite the fact that the pay-off of high-quality service/work can be very clearly quantified. Without quantification, it is difficult to justify the monetary cost of improvements or effecting changes. Measuring quality performance, whether it be the cost of quality, market-place performance, or levels of customer satisfaction, provides a basis for being able to establish priorities, and generates a momentum for change.

● The lack of measurement often means that, particularly in the early period of implementation, few benefits are visible, either to top management or to other levels within the organization. If people feel that they are not improving or progressing, it is inevitable that momentum will be lost and people will focus on other, more tangible issues, such as production or financial performance.

● With much of the early history of total quality centred on manufacturing processes and systems and based on the approach of a number of the quality gurus, one of the key reasons for problems in the implementation of total quality is the failure of many organizations to recognize the importance of people as the actual deliverers or doers in a total quality programme. The IPM report indicates that there is a growing recognition that there are many more human resource issues involved in a move to total quality than organizations had originally envisaged.[3] As has already been mentioned, people feel threatened by change, particularly major change. The result is that they will often pay lip-service to these changes without really altering their attitudes or their approach. There is a need to focus on management style, which I will deal with a little later, on the approach to training and development and on the different skills required which are core to human resource policies within organizations, as well as to consider such things as the performance management and payment systems.

● Related to this, there is often insufficient understanding of the state of morale within organizations, particularly in an environment of major change when there are likely to be fears about job security and even actual redundancies. While on the one hand, these can and have had a major impact on total quality programmes, there are examples where total quality has been used as the major business driver in order to achieve survival in a highly competitive situation. During the 1980s one major man-made fibres company did use total quality as the key business driver in a situation where price competition and over-capacity in the world market meant that cost reductions had to be carried out. Using a total quality approach, and despite a number of hiccups because of enforced redundancies, the company not only survived but remained the only European-based company to do so and compete with the Pacific basin. It required vision, leadership and keeping one's nerve as the workforce reacted badly to the redundancies. The key to success was that the total quality vision in the effort to survive was much more attractive at the end of the day than the more traditional cost reductions, even though both led to redundancies.

● There seems to be little evidence that trade union opposition or resistance to total quality initiatives has directly damaged, at least in the long term, any total quality programmes. This, to some extent, could be a reflection of the weakened trade union position during the 1980s and the early 1990s, coupled with the espousal of total quality by a number of high-profile trade union leaders. Nevertheless, there is some evidence that lack of co-operation from the trade unions has at least slowed down the momentum of some total quality programmes and possibly contributed, amongst many of the other factors raised above, to the lack of achievement of many of the programmes.

So what are the lessons for implementation based on the experience of the 1980s and early 1990s? The key points would seem to be:

● focus clearly the efforts associated with the early implementation of the total quality programme and build slowly
● measure, remeasure and never stop measuring in order to establish priorities – which will inevitably change as time passes – and to demonstrate tangible benefits
● build the commitment of the people within the organization and never stop focusing on the importance of their role within the overall programme – people learn by doing, so give them plenty of opportunity to do so.

The culture and structure of organizations

The experience of implementing total quality indicates that some of the biggest difficulties occur in large, hierarchial and often bureaucratic organizations. Yet such organizations are probably those which have the least customer focus and the greatest requirement for a total quality programme. They are often characterized by:

● Functional hierarchies with an emphasis on individual specialisms – 'my job', 'my area of responsibility' types of attitude. This has meant that individuals at all levels within organizations have tended to defend their own territory and the status quo and to resist the changes which are likely to be brought about by total quality. The biggest aspect of this change is that customer-orientation means that the whole organization has to focus on a 'horizontal' basis on the external customer, on product or service lines, not on individual specialisms or hierarchies.

● A lack of flexibility and a slowness to react to market changes, whereas total quality demands rapid reaction to customer requirements, which are likely to be changing constantly.

● Unclear and often incredibly slow decision-making processes. Within hierarchical organizations this is often a deliberate result of spreading or diluting responsibility and an aversion to people taking personal responsibility for their decisions or the results of their actions. Yet one of the fundamental tenets of total quality is personal responsibility for quality, whatever one's level in the organization.

● Over-engineered and bureaucratic processes which are often inward looking and are not sufficiently focused on business needs or customer requirements. This has often resulted from a tendency for such organizations to try and build 'perfect systems', which may satisfy the internal needs of the organization but do not reflect the reality in the market place.

With the competitive pressures brought about by the changes in world markets during the 1980s and 1990s, a great deal of action has been taken within such organizations to try and improve processes, to delayer the management hierarchy and to streamline bureaucracy. But this has not necessarily resulted in the changes in culture that are essential to the successful introduction of total quality. As mentioned before, the lack of success of total quality programmes in a number of such organizations probably stems from the fact that the organizations have not taken a sufficiently hard look at themselves and at the implications of total quality before embarking on the road to long-term implementation.

What lessons can be drawn from this experience? A number suggest themselves:

● Within the context of an overall vision and strategy, start the programme in one part or at the periphery of the organization. Do not try to take on the whole organization in one go but select a part that is led by someone enthusiastic for change and for total quality, where business results can be achieved reasonably quickly and where a momentum for change can be generated both for that unit and for the organization as a whole. It is essential that the business unit or units chosen are at the core of the business and are not seen as being unimportant to overall business success. One also has to be aware of the 'not invented here' syndrome as one tries to spread success.

● Ensure the whole approach is focused on the external customer, at least initially. While recognizing the importance of the customer–supplier links within the organization, the needs of the external customer must be paramount and be communicated as such. A number of organizations have demonstrated how this can be successfully achieved:

    – within British Airways there was the high-profile attendance by senior management and preaching of the message to everyone concerned at a long-running series of briefing workshops

    – British Telecom emphasized the importance of the needs of the external customer by means of various performance indicators that had high visibility to the external customer, such as the number of pay phones in operation as opposed to being out of order

    – more recently, the Post Office introduced performance indicators which did not, as previously, measure performance within the organization, such as the time it took for a letter to be processed from the point at which it arrived in the sorting office to the point at which it left. Instead, they introduced a measure which took account of delivery time from the point at which a letter was posted to the point at which it was delivered.

Fundamental to the approaches of these three organizations was the use of high-profile measures to spread the message that the external customer was key and that performance was measured in terms of external customer satisfaction.

● As the total quality programme develops in one part of the organization, it is important to spread the message about the benefits of the approach horizontally, firstly because it will provide peer group influence between different parts of the organization and secondly because it is necessary to break down the barriers between the various hierarchies by demonstrating that it's the cross-functional approach which is likely to yield results. Interestingly, one financial services organization, which had a large number of 'directors', decided that the best approach to total quality was to involve them as a complete group across the organization as a prelude to launching total quality to the rest of their staff. The prime purpose of this was to break down hierarchical barriers and provide a cross-functional approach to client service.

● Partly linked to the previous point, it is important that analysis and the establishment of measures are carried out on a cross-functional basis so that all concerned understand and 'buy into' the measures. This provides a much better pace for breaking down the traditional barriers between the various parts of a large organization and provides a framework for greater flexibility. It is also likely to enhance communication and begin to generate greater responsiveness to the market place.

In putting forward these four key lessons, I have not considered at this stage the issue of decision-making processes within such large organizations. My view is that you need to start breaking down the barriers, as indicated, without falling into the trap of talking about, or indeed trying to decentralize and introduce 'local empowerment'. All the evidence suggests that this would be seen as no more than a gimmick or a threat, without proper understanding of its implications. This can only come once people understand the issues and challenges brought about by total quality and begin to see the need for greater responsiveness, greater flexibility and quicker decision-making.

Management attitudes and actions

The third major area where problems occur in a total quality programme is that of management attitudes and actions. In implementing total quality, it has to be recognized that the initiative may be seen as a potential threat at all levels of management. At senior management level it demands public long-term commitment to fundamental change within the organization, while at middle management level it demands a radical revision of how they operate and a move away from their traditional hierarchical power.

Performance measures are a crucial aspect of the problem. Most of management will recognize, if pushed, that there are probably quality problems in some parts of the organization and that the organization does not always perform at its best in terms of customer satisfaction, even if there is no direct systematic evidence. However, traditionally, these same managers tend to have their own performance measured by factors other than those associated with total quality, such as financial performance measures or production performance measures. In other areas, particularly in functional support departments, there are often few direct performance measures and, in many cases, insufficient internal customer focus. Management attitudes, and indeed their behaviour, are likely to be shaped by the measures of performance which are applied to them. As one senior manager in a financial and professional services organization put it to me: 'I will respond to those factors which are likely to cause me difficulties with my superiors, and if they tend to be internally oriented performance measures, then I will respond even though I know that this is not really the priority.' In other words, the performance measures used in an organization are the primary determinants of management behaviour, whatever top management may say should happen.

As has been stated throughout this book, the commitment of

senior and middle management is critical to shaping the success of the total quality programme, and yet the evidence would suggest that a number of difficulties occur during implementation:

● The survey carried out for the IPM report revealed that 67% of those responding had experienced problems in the implementation of total quality, particularly as regards restructuring and management change[4] – thus confirming that it is in the area of management that some of the biggest difficulties occur.

● There is a lack of real commitment to the total quality programme amongst senior management. This is a difficult area because at the beginning of all programmes senior management will recognize the importance of the total quality programme and apparently commit to it. What then seems to happen is that top management fail to understand that their own behaviour and the behaviour of everyone in the organization must change if the total quality programme is to be successful. Some of those associated with the implementation of total quality report that in many cases organizations end up buying a training programme and measuring their progress by the number trained and how many training sessions have been run. The primary problem, however, is that top management do not seem to understand the implications of the culture and attitude change associated with a total quality programme. Clearly, in the long run, the implementation of total quality is concerned with better business results, but it is unlikely to provide the major short-term results on which much of top management will focus.

● Surprisingly, managers generally are often unaware of the real quality problems within their organizations. Their overall view of performance is often determined by the fact that they have not received a huge number of complaints. Yet the evidence suggests that the majority of unhappy customers never bother to complain about shoddy products or services in a manner that lets management know that there is a problem. Customers will often allow themselves to be fobbed off and are not aware of the formal channels for providing feedback on a particular product or service. This same group of customers, however, may influence the market image of the organization by sharing their complaints with other current or would-be customers. The reality is that there is little systematic customer feedback, unless associated with a total quality programme, and this tip-of-the-iceberg phenomenon enables management to come to the conclusion that their performance is 'not too bad' and that the quality of their products and services is acceptable. This self-delusion can often cause them to conclude that total quality is simply the current 'flavour of the month', which will be replaced by another fad next month. They will not bother, therefore, to buy into the concept.

● The power and status of management, particularly at the middle management level, are likely to be changed from the more traditional mould as a result of total quality. Total quality demands that the role of management is to create the framework within which quality problems can be resolved and an attitude of continuous improvement can permeate throughout the organization. This means that the traditional management role is likely to change into a much more enabling and facilitating role, coaching individuals and giving them the tools or opportunity to make changes. This significant change of emphasis is not only likely to prove a threat to middle management, but in many cases they are unlikely to be equipped to carry out this radically different role. This in turn will make them more fearful of the changes.

● By endeavouring to break down functional barriers and by emphasizing the importance of the overall team effort, total quality renders the culture of the 'individual' inappropriate within the organization. Success is dependent on cross-functional, cross-boundary working with an emphasis on teams. This provides a potential threat to management, where individual performance is traditionally considered of higher value than working in teams.

● Linked to the previous point, in most organizations that have not applied total quality, the performance management system is based on individual working and individual performance measures. The evidence would suggest that as a total quality programme is implemented, the performance management measures are often not changed sufficiently quickly, partly because of the need to ensure that short-term financial or production performance continues. This provides mixed messages from management and does not emphasize the importance of the total quality measures.

● On a more basic note, there has to be a recognition that even if it is possible to set new targets associated with the total quality programme and to gain commitment for the implementation of the new programme, this tends to create even greater workloads for an already over-stretched resource. Failure to provide adequate resources to support management, or failure to change responsibilities so that management are freed up to support the total quality programme, often provide significant barriers to success.

● Other issues associated with management, which also cause problems in the implementation of a total quality programme, include lack of clarity about the management structure, too much bureaucracy (which leads to lack of personal responsibility on the part of management) and considerable emphasis on short-termism.

The experiences of the 1980s and early 1990s have demonstrated that management attitudes and actions can cause significant difficulties in the implementation of a total quality programme. Many of the actions required to resolve these difficulties have been outlined in the S-P-O approach but seem to require further reinforcement:

● Top management's role is to create a framework for change and to demonstrate by clear actions that change will take place. These actions should include:
  – changes and additions to performance measures which take account of the requirements of the total quality programme
  – clear responsibility for the total quality programme at top management level – either by the appointment of someone at this level to take responsibility for the programme or by including it in the existing responsibilities of a particular top manager. Above all, it must fall to someone who has a clear personal commitment to the implementation of total quality.

● General or divisional managers should have overall and clear responsibility for implementation and should be involved in:

- the design of the implementation programme, developing the detailed components and milestones within an overall framework created by top management
- the establishment of mechanisms to provide them with a framework for action and which are not too centralized or too standardized. For instance, mechanisms for obtaining customer feedback, whether internal or external, are necessary to ensure meeting different customer needs and to reflect the different operations of the organization
- the establishment of quality-oriented performance measures for all individual parts of the organization
- the emphasis on building new skills amongst management which allow them to take on facilitating and enabling roles.

● The performance measurement system is likely to require fundamental change in order to incorporate measures reflecting the needs of the total quality programme, as follows:
  - reviewing the reward system to ensure it supports the objectives of the total quality programme
  - revising the performance review system to ensure performance management objectives are in line with the objectives of the total quality programme
  - carrying out a fundamental review of the skill needs for all levels of management to ensure training and development processes reflect the new skills required
  - changing the management development processes to reflect the fact that the organization is moving towards a culture of learning, self-development and continuous improvement.

Measuring success

There are two themes which run consistently through this book, the importance of measurement and the importance of getting the commitment of people in any total quality programme. Two recent developments reinforce this and provide a framework for the 1990s – the establishment in 1992 of the European Quality Award and the development of Investors in People within the UK.

The European Quality Award

In 1988, 14 leading Western European businesses took the initiative of forming the European Foundation for Quality Management (EFQM) in recognition of the potential for competitive advantage through the application of total quality. By October 1992, membership had grown to over 230 members from most Western European countries and most business sectors. The role of the EFQM is to enhance the position of Western European businesses in the world market in the following ways:

- accelerating the acceptance of quality as a strategy for global competitive advantage
- stimulating and assisting the deployment of quality improvement activities.

The EFQM, with the support of the European Organization for Quality and the European Commission, took a leading role in establishing the European Quality Award in recognition of the achievement of organizations in pursuing total quality. The award was presented for the first time in 1992. It incorporates European quality prizes, awarded to organizations that demonstrate excellence in the management of quality as their fundamental process for continuous improvement, and the European Quality Award, which is awarded to the most successful exponent of total quality management in Western Europe. The first winner of the award was Xerox.

While the award provides a high profile for total quality, its importance is more in the self-appraisal process associated with determining how organizations are progressing in total quality, and which involves a regular and systematic review of organizations' activities and results. This process allows organizations to identify their strengths and the areas in which improvements can be made.

The self-appraisal process is based on the European TQM model:

> Processes are the means by which the organization harnesses and releases the talents of its people to produce results. In other words, the processes and the people are the **Enablers** which provide the **Results.**

Expressed graphically, the principle looks like this:

Figure 35 The European TQM Model

Leadership	People management	Processes	People satisfaction	Business results
	Policy and strategy		Customer satisfaction	
	Resources		Impact on society	

Enablers ⟶   ⟵ **Results** ⟶

This model was developed as a framework for the European Quality Award, but provides a method of self-appraisal for organizations by identifying nine elements which can determine an organization's progress towards total quality management. These nine elements are as follows:

Enablers

Leadership – the behaviour of all managers in driving the organization towards total quality

Policy and strategy – the organization's mission, values, vision and strategic direction and the ways in which the organization achieves them

People management – the management of the organization's people and how the organization releases the full potential of its people to improve its business continuously

Resources – the management utilization and preservation of resources and how the organization's resources are effectively deployed in support of policy and strategy

Processes – the management of all the value-adding activities within the organization and how processes are identified, reviewed and, if necessary, revised to ensure continuous improvement of the organization's business

Results

Customer satisfaction – what the perception of external customers is of the organization and of its products and services

People satisfaction – what the people's feelings are about their organization

Impact on society – what the perception of the organization is within society at large. This includes views on the organization's approach to quality of life, the environment and to the preservation of global resources

Business results – what the organization is achieving in relation to its planned business performance, in terms of both financial and non-financial measures.

Interestingly, this self-appraisal links directly back to the strategy and planning elements of S-P-O outlined earlier in this book. The full self-appraisal process associated with the European Quality Award provides guidelines for identifying and addressing total quality issues and enables organizations to establish measures whereby they can determine their progress and, more importantly, deal with problems or blockages.

Investors in People

Investors in People is a national standard introduced in the early 1990s within the UK. It is designed to demonstrate whether an organization invests in its people as part of its overall business strategy. Although not directly linked to total quality, it does provide a framework which recognizes the importance of people in achieving organizational goals. If a key element of the business strategy is the introduction and development of total quality, then there is a more direct link between Investors in People and the total quality programme. As with the European Quality Award, the value of Investors in People lies not just in achieving the required standard and kitemark associated with it but, more importantly, in the self-appraisal process, which measures performance against certain national standards, identifies gaps and enables the people element of any business strategy to be integrated into that strategy.

The national standards associated with Investors in People are as follows:

● an Investor in People makes a public commitment from the top of the organization to develop all employees to achieve its business objectives

- an Investor in People regularly reviews the training and development needs of all its employees
- an Investor in People takes action to train and develop individuals on recruitment and throughout their employment
- an Investor in People evaluates the investment in training and development to assess achievement and improve future effectiveness.

The concept of continuous improvement built into this approach and the focus on people as a key part of business strategy are clearly linked to quality and provide a method not only of measuring success but of linking people into that success as a fundamental prerequisite.

The self-appraisals linked to the European Quality Award and Investors in People provide a basis for measurement, evaluation and continuous improvement – the heart of the total quality process.

Conclusions

As already indicated, the evidence suggests that many organizations will fail to implement a total quality programme successfully or fail to maintain its momentum in the long term. The frustrating thing about this is that top management, and organizations generally, know, and have been told at length by the many gurus on total quality, how they should set about implementing a total quality programme. They fail because they do not take on board that total quality is for the long term and requires fundamental changes in culture. It is not enough to introduce new processes and new structures without recognizing the key issue of culture change. The challenge for management is to overcome the natural tendency for short-termism and to move to a culture of long-term continuous improvement. This and this alone has the capacity to change business performance and enhance profitability in the long term.

Chapter 16
EVALUATION OF RESULTS

The full cycle of S-P-O has now been described, taking an organization from the initial strategy to complete implementation. Long-term success is dependent on the continuous working of this cycle to ensure that a climate of continuous improvement is maintained and developed. Reaching Crobsy's final stage of certainty takes a long time and, as Philips has highlighted, reaching excellence may take up to 20 years. Once a total quality programme is implemented there must be continuous evaluation of results to monitor the success (or failure) of every aspect of the programme. Achieving this requires the use of similar tools described during the strategy development stage of the process and includes in particular:

- a re-evaluation of quality costs
- a check on attitudes throughout the organization
- continuous and close evaluation of customer requirements
- a survey of the effectiveness of the task groups and improvement groups.

Quality costs

At the strategy stage of the total quality programme an analysis of quality costs was carried out under the following main headings:

- costs of prevention
- costs of appraisal
- costs of internal failure
- costs of external failure.

As part of the evaluation process the base costs which have been established at the strategy stage should be reviewed to determine what progress has been made since the implementation of the total quality programme.

People and attitudes

The organization climate survey has established a base for measuring the climate at the start of the programme. As indicated in Chapter 9, this can be used to update the prevailing climate within an organization by regular completion of the survey questionnaire. This enables management in particular to concentrate on any areas which may be causing difficulty or to highlight problems which are occurring and need resolution.

Customer requirements

Customer requirements do not remain static, nor does the actual client/customer base of an organization. As a result, during the evaluation process a customer/client survey needs to be carried out to determine the performance of the organization. This should be backed up by regular meetings with the key clients/customers in order to strengthen the relationship, and at the same time the changing requirements of customers/clients can be more easily identified through this dialogue. Part of this process should also involve at departmental level the review of roles and responsibilities and the key targets for each individual department which has been carried out at the strategy development stage. Again this process is not static. It needs continuous renewal and certainly the minimum requirement is that such a review of objectives on a departmental and individual basis is carried out annually.

The whole review process also needs to be linked with some definitive measure of customer satisfaction, such as a measure of the number of customer complaints being received.

Improvement group/task group evaluation

In a total quality programme with the emphasis on hard results in terms of improved quality performance there is a danger that the actual performance of task groups and improvement groups is not properly measured. It can be argued that the very success of the groups in terms of completed projects is sufficient measure of the general progress within the total quality programme. This can be

Figure 36 Improvement Group Audit Checklist

GENERAL

1 List those factors which have *helped* the introduction of improvement groups.

2 List those factors which have *hindered* the introduction of improvement groups.

3 Are you satisified with the progress of improvement groups? – please explain your answer.

4 Do you think the improvement groups have benefited
  – the company?
  – the employees?
  Please give details.

5 What are the main achievements of the improvement group programme?

DETAILED EVALUATION

A *Organization*

1 Are the arrangements for meetings satisfactory in
  – location?
  – equipment?
  – timing?

2 Are meetings held regularly according to the weekly schedule?

3 Are there any difficulties in attending meetings?

4 Who collects data – leaders, members or both?

B *Leadership*

1 Does the leadership of the improvement group work satisfactorily?

2 Are opinions of *all* members taken into account?

C *Management*

1 Does your manager support your improvement group? If so, how?

2 What response have you received to your proposals?

3 Have there been difficulties in implementing your proposals? If so, give details.

4 Do you consider you have top management support?

D *Communication*

1 Was the initial briefing about improvement groups sufficient?

2 Are *all* employees kept briefed about the work of improvement groups?

3 Do you consider there should be any further communication about improvement groups?

E *Facilitator*

1 Is the level of support from the facilitator sufficient?

2 What further support (if any) do you require?

3 Can the facilitator be contacted easily?

F *Training*

1 Was the initial training sufficient?

2 What further training do you think is necessary?

THE FUTURE

1 What views do you have on the future success of improvement groups?

2 What should be done to strengthen further the improvement group programme?

3 Should there be regular review meetings to monitor progress? If so, please give details.

dangerously misleading because it is not difficult to achieve short-
term progress within an organization provided a total quality programme has been properly introduced and a certain momentum
generated.

The facilitator has a responsibility to review on a regular basis
the performance of improvement groups and it is important for the
total quality manager to carry out similar reviews of performance
of task groups. In order to do this in an objective way it is useful to
carry out a small survey based on a checklist approach. Details of
the checklist are set out in Figure 36.

The checklist should form a basis for discussion in separate
groups of departmental management, middle management,
supervision/group leaders and the individual groups. I have found
that it is not especially helpful to use the checklist as a basis for a
questionnaire because much of its usefulness arises from the discussion between the facilitator (or the consultant carrying out the
survey) and the individual groups. Additionally, as indicated, it is
helpful to carry out the review by having discussions with the
different peer groups. This usually enables a full and frank discussion on the progress being achieved and any difficulties that arise.
Once the review has been carried out the facilitator, total quality
manager or the consultant should produce a short report which
includes:

- a general overview of progress to date
- successes achieved
- significant problems identified
- action plan for the future.

The evaluation of a total quality programme should not take place
just after the initial introduction of the programme but on a regular, probably annual, basis. The full report of the evaluation in its
various constituent parts looking at costs of quality, people and
attitudes, customer requirements and the performance of task
groups and improvement groups should be presented to the steering committee and also to the board or management committee.
This report should form the basis for the future progress of the
programme for the next six to twelve months and in particular
should assist in:

- identifying improvements that can be made to the programme

- redirecting the strategy to concentrate on areas of concern such as the need to concentrate on particular customer requirements or to extend the training to include specialized groups or techniques
- identifying in overall terms any further 'development gaps' which require rectification
- determining the extent to which a programme is extended and developed, particularly in relation to new task groups or additional improvement groups.

This regular review process is no more than good management practice and should not be unique to the total quality programme. Nevertheless there is a great deal of evidence to suggest that once a programme is established in the West there is a tendency to move on to the next programme or 'flavour of the month' and allow the existing programme to manage itself. This will not work with a total quality programme, as is so forcefully put by Deming, Juran, Crosby and others and so well demonstrated by the Japanese in creating the cycle of continuous improvement. It also provides a litmus test for senior management by giving them the opportunity to develop forward strategy and at the same time demonstrate their longer-term commitment to the programme.

Rewards

This long-term commitment is not only maintained by carrying out the regular review of progress but by ensuring that there is considerable publicity about the programme and especially about its successes. There is often much discussion about the extent to which management should recognize an individual's or a group's special efforts in the overall total quality programme and how this should be done. The debate centres on two aspects, firstly the issue of whether there should be a special award or not and secondly, if there are to be awards, what type of award should apply?

In the Japanese context there is a great deal of emphasis on recognition through special prizes and awards. At a national level the so-called Deming Prize, *the* prime prize for quality performance in Japan, is probably the most coveted industrial and commercial award there is. This is supported from national level through regional level right down to individual company and departmental level. The rewards are based on recognition and publicity and usually have minimal material value, and provide a great deal of kudos to those who receive them. In some cases it is an indirect award, such as the opportunity to travel. For instance, Sony Corporation have a worldwide quality circle convention which brings together the 'best' circles from around the world from time to time in Tokyo.

Outside the Japanese context, however, this emphasis on recognition has mixed responses. Within the UK there are now quality awards at national level and within individual companies there are awards recognizing special merit in terms of quality performance. At shop floor level within the UK there is considerable ambivalence to such awards. For instance, within the male mass toiletries organization, when carrying out the total quality programme audit it became apparent that there was positive resentment among the improvement group members to having special awards for the most outstanding improvement group in any one year. This was considered divisive with a strong feeling emerging that any such awards would in the end be counterproductive. On the other hand, within a major financial services organization there was strong support for special awards to the improvement groups for their outstanding contribution.

My own view is that special awards for merit in making an outstanding contribution to a total quality programme can help the programme a great deal by providing a vehicle for regular, probably annual, publicity about the programme. In general, people do like to have their contribution publicized in company newspapers and the concept of a regular award ceremony provides this opportunity.

The second issue raised is: what type of awards should be made? During the introduction of total quality programmes the question is often asked whether an existing suggestion scheme should now be regarded as defunct, and whether in future there would be no monetary award for making proposals to improve performance under the total quality programme. Where suggestion schemes are in existence there is likely to be some pressure for direct monetary reward on the basis of 'why should management get all the benefit?' Some organizations have in fact allowed improvement groups to submit projects through the suggestion scheme process but this has tended to cause problems because suggestion schemes are designed essentially for individuals, rather than groups.

The issue of monetary reward can sometimes be a difficult question to answer unless an environment has been created where there is recognition by all those involved in a total quality programme that quality is everybody's business and that the success and indeed the survival of the organization is based on the overall quality performance. Additionally, unlike suggestion schemes, it is difficult to identify clearly which individual or indeed which group has actually produced a solution which merits a special monetary reward. I find, however, that the issue of a direct monetary reward tends to be raised at the beginning of a programme but that once the programme is underway people recognize that everybody is involved and therefore it is impossible to reward an individual or group. In the final analysis, provided the briefing on the programme is carried out properly, the issue of direct monetary reward tends to resolve itself.

Apart from the monetary reward there are nevertheless opportunities to provide rewards to individual groups for outstanding performance. In general I do not think that individual awards should be made and believe that the majority should be on the basis of groups who have contributed in some way to the total quality programme. Within organizations, possible approaches can include:

- an annual company quality award which is given on a departmental basis and recognizes the most improved quality performance against some defined base in a 12 month period
- a 'best' improvement group award which recognizes the outstanding project of the year done by an improvement group. This is sometimes a difficult award to measure but provided some broad guidelines are set in terms of the most orginal, the one that provides the highest savings, the one that contributed most to the improvement quality, then it can be well received – similar awards can also be given to task groups.

In my view much more important than individual awards is the publicity surrounding a total quality programme. Management demonstrate their commitment not by giving awards but by being actively involved in the programme. I have already made reference to the outstanding contribution made by the seafoods board in attending major presentations by their improvement groups and participating directly in the programme. Within the constraints of size and practicality it is possible to set up top management meetings with direct participants in the total quality programme as part of the involvement process. This is participative management at its best and provides a visible means of demonstrating top management commitment. Other examples of publicizing the total quality programme include:

- a 'total quality day' made up of exhibitions and stands emphasizing the quality performance during the previous 12 months
- often linked to the total quality day, open days for the families of employees to attend and see some of the major quality achievements
- regular campaign posters with the total quality message or reinforcement of particular themes. For instance, within the male mass toiletries organization the total quality programme came under the heading of 'PRIDE'. Everywhere in the organization there were signs and PRIDE messages which reinforced the message constantly
- regular publicity on successful projects in company newspapers and on noticeboards also helps to create the environment that success breeds success.

The basic message is comparatively simple. A total quality programme needs to be regularly evaluated in order to create an environment for continuous improvement. The evaluation itself also provides a foundation for major publicity coupled with awards for success. This creates an environment of continuous improvement and generates a culture within an organization where quality is not only considered to be important but can be demonstrated to be so through continuous success.

Chapter 17
THE QUALITY ACTION LIST

Successful implementation of total quality is based on following the S-P-O approach. Determining whether an organization is meeting the criteria for success can be achieved quickly by asking the following key questions under the main headings of the S-P-O approach.

Strategy development

- Do you know what the costs of quality are within your organization?
- Do you know what the costs of quality are within your particular area of responsibility?
- What changes for the better or worse have been achieved in the cost of quality over the past 12 months?
- What systems have been put into place to measure the cost of quality on a regular basis?
- When did you last measure the organizational climate within the organization?
- What views do management and the work force have on the total quality programme?
- What management organization has been put in place in order to meet the requirements of the total quality programme?
- What are the prevailing attitudes towards customers/clients?
- How would you define the customer requirements in terms of external customers?
- How would you define the customer requirements in terms of your immediate internal customers?
- When did you last carry out a market survey to determine customer requirements?

- When did you last meet your customers/clients?
- How would you define your customers'/clients' view of the organization and your own departments?

Planning

- Who is the board level person responsible for the total quality programme?
- How would you define his/her responsibilities?
- Who is the full time senior manager with specific responsibility for the total quality programme?
- How would you define his/her responsibilities?
- Is there a steering committee within your organization?
- Who are its members?
- What are the training programmes which have been set up as a direct result of the total quality programme?
- Do they cover training and development of
  - top management
  - management
  - task group leaders
  - improvement group leaders
  - facilitators?
- Has a detailed timetable for implementing the total quality programme been established?
- What are its main components?

Operating elements

- What are the details of the briefing programme?
- What are the components of the briefing pack?
- Does the briefing programme involve everybody from top management right down to the shop floor?
- Does the main training programme incorporate training in
  - concepts of quality
  - interpersonal skills
  - statistical and systematic problem solving techniques?
- Is there a facilitator responsible for the improvement group process?

- What are the main responsibilities of the facilitator in terms of task groups and improvement groups?
- In the improvement groups:
  - **WHO** – manages them?
    - – teaches them?
    - – introduces them?
    - – facilitates them?
    - – leads them?
    - – belongs to them?
    - – does not belong to them?
    - – selects the members?
    - – selects the leaders?
    - – identifies problems for the groups?
    - – measures their performance?
  - **WHAT** – are they?
    - – do they do?
    - – will it do for the organization and the people in it?
    - – times do they meet?
    - – training is involved?
    - – commitment is needed?
    - – problems are worked on?
  - **WHY** – should they meet?
    - – are improvement groups voluntary?
    - – are improvement groups led by supervisors?
    - – do they meet in company time?
    - – are they so training oriented?
    - – are they so structured?
    - – should they be measured?
  - **WHEN** – do they meet?
    - – are they measured?
    - – are they stopped?
- What arrangements are there for evaluation of progress including a review of:
  - – costs of quality
  - – people and attitudes
  - – improvement group/task group performance
- What arrangements are there for publicizing the successes in the total quality programme?
- Are there any special awards associated with the total quality programme?

Figure 37 Implementing Total Quality

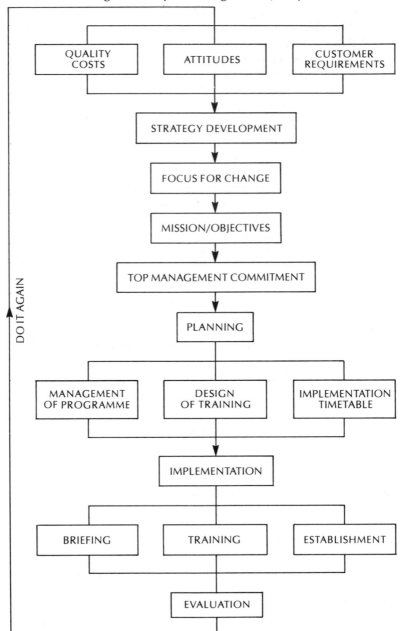

This checklist provides the basis of the total quality programme. Unless organizations or those responsible for the programme are able to provide definitive answers to this list then there is the likelihood that the programme may have its faults. Implementing total quality requires an integrated approach based on the S-P-O principle set out in Figure 37.

Total quality is recognized by all as being the key to the future of individual organizations. It is recognized, as it has been in the ODI survey of chief executives, that total quality is about management and in particular about participative management. Without participation, without dialogue within organizations, without listening to clients and customers, total quality will never be achieved. Total quality is also about changes in the way of thinking, the behaviour and the culture within organizations. As the Japanese have so successfully demonstrated, total quality is about shared values and motivating everybody in the organization from top to bottom to maintain and keep to the highest quality standards.

But the message of total quality goes much further than the individual organizations that make up each country's economy. With the single market being achieved in Europe in 1992, standards must be maintained across the whole of Europe, not only to maintain the economic base of the single market, but to defend itself directly against the standards set by the Japanese over the last 20 to 30 years.

In simple terms total quality is about attitudes, a way of life, achieving excellence. It is about success through people. The alternative within organizations and within Europe as a whole is not only to lose out competitively but to fail together as the Japanese and the Pacific Basin overtake us.

References

Chapter 1
1 ODI, *Total Quality: The ODI Survey* (Bristol, ODI Ltd, 1987)

Chapter 2
1 Philip B. Crosby, *Quality is Free* (McGraw-Hill, 1978)

Chapter 3
1 Ron Collard, 'The Quality Circle in Context', *Personnel Management*, September 1981
2 IDS, *Flexibility at Work*, Study No. 360 (London, IDS, April 1986)

Chapter 4
1 Yoshinobu Hattori, 'TQC in Japan's Distribution and Service Industries', *Dentsu Japan Marketing/Advertising* Autumn 1984 (Volume II No. 4)
2 Peter Wickens, *The Road to Nissan: Flexibility, Quality, Teamwork* (London, Macmillan, 1988)

Chapter 6
1 DTI, *Standards, Quality and International Competitiveness*, Cmnd 8621 (London, DTI, 1986)

Chapter 7
1 R. J. Mortiboys (for the DTI), *Quality Management: A Guide for Chief Executives* (London, DTI, 1986)

Chapter 9
1 T. J. Peters and Robert H. Waterman, *In Search of Excellence: Lessons from America's Best-Run Companies* (New York, Harper and Row, 1982)
2 J. Cullen and J. Hollingum, *Implementing Total Quality* (Bedford, IFS Publications/Springer-Verlag, 1987)
3 Peter Wickens, *The Road to Nissan* (London, Macmillan, 1988)

Chapter 11

1 A. V. Feigenbaum, *Total Quality Control* (New York, McGraw-Hill, 1983)

Chapter 15

1 T. J. Peters, *Customer Revolution* video (BBC Education and Training Sales, 1989)
2 Institute of Personnel Management, *Quality: People Management Matters* (London, IPM, 1993)
3 *ibid.*
4 *ibid.*

Index